Piggy Bank Blues

How To Make Money While You Look For a Job
A Step-by-Step Workbook

by Donna D. Buskirk

Published by Donna D. Buskirk
OneAmericanWriter.com
Copyright © 2010 by Donna Dickason Buskirk

Cover art by James Gray of EndlessBounty.com.
Cover design by Tia Gray. (Portfolio: Tia.EndlessBounty.com)

Scripture quotations, unless noted otherwise, are taken from the Holy Bible: New International Version®. NIV®. Copyright © 1973, 1978, 1984, International Bible Society. Used by permission of Zondervan Bible Publishers. All rights reserved.

All content is for informational purposes only and is **NOT** intended as legal or professional advice, and cannot replace advice from a licensed professional who considers all specific facts and circumstances applicable in any specific situation. Contact an attorney, insurance professional, and/or local government office for advice about your particular situation.

WWW.OneAmericanWriter.com
ISBN 1453774408
EAN-13 9781453774403

Contents

Here's to you!

This book is dedicated to my husband, who shall remain nameless – he knows who he is. I couldn't have done this without him. He believes in me. I can't wait to see how *his* projects turn out. Check his/our progress at DivinityVines.com. Here's to you, my love!

To Jessie, Anna and Jonathan, thanks for putting up with me saying, "Not now, I'm *writing*!" You're the greatest, and I'm the only Mom on the entire planet who gets you for kids. I can't *wait* to see what you do. Be good!

Special thanks to Chuck Lehning for sharing your story with readers!

Thanks to James and Tia Gray for the gift of your original art, but mostly, thank you for your friendship, your prayers, your music, and your sharing hearts. Many thanks to Teresa Smith of Harry's Market (MeetMeAtHarrys.com) for encouragement from the heart, and for so many warm introductions to local folks. And Molly Keppler, of Keppler Landscaping and Calico Farm in Chapel Hill, North Carolina, thank you for your friendship, for the chickens and goats and wisdom to go with them, and for editing this manuscript. Let's work together again!

To my readers, it may not be fair, but it is often easier to find a new job when you are currently employed than when you are unemployed. Show potential employers that you are a person of action by turning a hobby into a sideline business or by providing a service in your community or online.

As you work through this workbook, blog about your field of expertise or network in your community to establish your credibility and to discover a need you can meet.

Guard your courage carefully. Counteract every discouraging thought with positive actions and *press forward*.

Foreword

It's 3:30 in the morning and I've been up since two. My online job search is frustrating lately because clicking "Apply Now" takes me to registration pages and pop-up ads for universities and work-at-home schemes. I feel like singing the blues.

If I could sing, I suppose I would try to do that for a living, but no one earns a living with talent alone. (If a writer writes, but no one reads the pages, does the keyboard make noise?) You must market yourself and do a dozen things right to make it work. This book will help.

They say you should follow your passion, but as one friend asks, "What about this -- what if your passion *is* working for yourself? What if you knock on doors to find lawn-mowing clients, and you work hard enough to eventually hire help, and you get to be your own boss?"

I think we should do work for which we get paid right away. For many of us, that might mean finding a part-time job until we find the next full-time opportunity. Some of us will work for ourselves like we always said we wanted to. One gentleman I read about was forced to retire in his sixties and was hired again in his seventies but while he waited, he stayed informed about his industry, he maintained his professional contacts, and he stayed in top physical condition.

Not many of us can sing the blues for a living, and none of us can sing the blues for long if we want to stay encouraged. Change your thinking, take a deep breath, relax, make positive changes in your routine, and then go out and make something good happen. This *is* a time full of opportunities.

Forerhyme

I made a new word. After the foreword, here are two rhymes that fit perfectly right here, in the "forerhyme." What I love about independent publishing is that you can make your own rules. As you begin working for yourself, use that freedom wisely. Use standards of excellence while remembering that, if you tend to be a perfectionist, "good enough" can be a valuable concept.

Fear can get in your way. It is easy to get discouraged when you work alone. Here is a motivational rhyme I wrote that is apt for job-seekers *and* business-starters. Please feel free to pass this on.

Accomplish It
Life is short, said the report
Make strong the defenses around your fort.
When enemy Discouragement tries to get in
Action cures fear, don't let him in!

Positive action will win the day
When Discouragement tries to block your way.
Thoughts of winning can help you, too.
Your thinking can change what you can do.

Tell Discouragement, "Cowardly liar,
I see you for what you are!
Pretending friendship, you spread this lie,
`You won't reach your goal, why even try?'"

Friend Accomplishment, come by me.
From Discouragement, set me free!
Accomplishment, tell me what I can do
I will take my orders from you!

Blues without a Tune

A few days ago, I was talking with a soccer dad at practice. He said, "I worked at the mill for 22 years. They flew some of the employees over to China to train our replacements. They closed the mill."

He went to school to learn an agricultural trade. He found a job recently and hopes they will give him more hours than he is currently working.

Once we simplify our lives and consolidate living arrangements if we must, let's look at this as a time full of opportunities. What new skills can you learn? What service can you provide to start a home-based business? Let's do more than make ends meet. Let's define new beginnings and earn success along the way.

As we help our families and neighbors, one vital thing we can share is encouragement. Here's hoping the following rhyme makes this point: Even if the economy doesn't improve soon, *we as individuals* can improve today and every day.

Piggy Bank Blues

I got the piggy bank blues and news you can use
It ain't gettin' better real soon.
We got men on the moon and China will soon
But it ain't gettin' better any time soon.

I got the piggy bank blues so I have to choose
Between food and gas and I have to take a pass
On the offer on TV to get the things
I used to be able to buy – I got the piggy bank
blues.

I'll let the economy slide down around me
I can't take it with me anyway.
Stuff I do have and don't have doesn't define me
So I don't think I can use those piggy bank blues.

I'll be wise and downsize voluntarily before circumstances force me down.
If you're lookin' for me at the mall or the movies, you won't find me there.
I'll be home growin' food in my own dang yard singing,
"They ain't gettin' me, those piggy bank blues!"

In-box

> **From:** Big Bad Boss
>   **To:** You
> **Subject: You don't *WHAT*?**
>
> Look, I don't care if you don't FEEL like getting up, or calling your best friend, or starting that project you told yourself you'd start.
>
> DO IT ANYWAY. Feelings *follow* actions.
>
> Knowing things will get better might not make you FEEL better right now. BUT DOING SOMETHING WILL.
>
> Build a dollhouse, mow a lawn, scrub the floor, clean the windows, write an essay, learn a craft, teach a class, help a neighbor.
>
> We need to work to feel whole.
>
> Your increased confidence might make all the difference in relationships, in a job search, in a business.

Chapter 1: It Happened to Me

My neighbor has a friend who has been out of work for two years. She and her husband put their house on the market because they could no longer afford to pay the mortgage. Then her husband was laid off from *his* job.

Another neighbor was laid off after ten years at a large pharmaceutical company. She has continued to work for that same company as a contractor, but she doesn't know how long that job situation will last.

Our friend Bob was laid off from his telecommunications job over three years ago. He has been making ends meet by doing some physical labor and some technical work, and now one of the part-time engineering jobs has turned into an excellent career move because his employer received a contract that will allow Bob to work full time. In the meantime, his kids pitch in by working and his wife works an extra job.

As for me, I was laid off after ten years at MCI, after WorldCom bought the company and got us on the evening news. After a few dicey months, I found a contract job as a technical writer at a smaller company, and when they offered me a permanent position, I felt comfortable enough with my boss to ask, "What's the point?" He assured me that layoffs would not happen at this company. The company had wonderful benefits and very caring upper management, so when they were bought by their largest competitor, the staff was in more shock than we were at MCI where annual staff reductions were the norm.

What can I say to people who are losing their homes or who can't pay the rent for two months in a row? When Kannapolis-based Pillowtex Corp shut down in 2003 near my home near Raleigh, NC, that nearby town lost its primary employer. What can I say to someone who worked hard for that company for over twenty or thirty years and might have to relocate to search for new work?

I remember thinking when I was younger, that people who say they can't find work but are unwilling to work at McDonald's shouldn't be entitled to receive unemployed benefits. Now that I've been in that situation myself – having to decide when to take a lower-paying job – I take back everything I ever thought or said. I want this book to help fill in the gap between jobs in some small way.

What a terrible decision to have to make. Do you take a job that won't pay enough to make ends meet, but that will at least keep food on the table, or do you keep looking for a job in your field? Once you take that lower-paying job, how will you have time to continue your job search? And how can you make an honest commitment to your employer if you only plan to stay until you find a more professional position?

In fact, when employers are legitimately concerned about hiring over-qualified candidates, it can be devastating to the men and women who hear once again that they did not land the position because they are overqualified. In many, many cases, those job-seekers would become dedicated, enthusiastic employees for years to come.

I hope that taking the steps in the workbook will help you to make the money you need during your job hunt without having to choose a lower-paying job. When you spend half or most of the day providing a needed service by following the steps in this workbook, and you devote the rest of the day to your ongoing search for employment, here are the benefits I hope you will enjoy:

- Satisfaction that only comes from working.
- New friendships and professional contacts in your community.
- The ability to organize your day with a productive routine as you set your own work schedule.
- The ability to smile easily again.

You may find that working for yourself is more secure than putting all of your eggs in one basket with a single employer.

God or People

I remember thinking when I was between jobs, "I'll have to trust God to help me, or ask my parents for help." When my parents pitched in to pay several mortgage payments, at first I felt like God had let me down. Now I know that it was God providing *through* my parents. But I spent over half of my life firmly believing God was fiction for people who needed a crutch, and I well remember how I hated "God-talk" at that time, so I won't include it here. You can read more about how faith gets me through and can get *you* through in the appendix.

What Did Bob Do?

My friend Bob, a laid-off telecommunications engineer, was helping us lay a new floor in our kitchen when I asked him what information he could share with the readers of this book.

"The best thing to do is to look for a part-time job or some side work to meet people and to make money to help with expenses. It doesn't pay a lot of money, but you can take pride in something. And you get a chance to meet people who can help you look for a job, too."

"I was hauling engines around and I threw my shoulder out and had to have surgery, so it was a good idea, but it turned out to be disastrous. You've got to be careful." This is a warning well heeded by those of us accustomed to sitting behind desks all day.

It Happened Again!

I have now been laid off for the third time. When I was laid off from the small company I mentioned above, I moved directly into a higher-paying position at *another* small firm. That company was bought twice.

There were no staff reductions the first time we were purchased, but, as you will read momentarily, the corporate giant that eventually bought us laid dozens of my coworkers and me off in the middle of the worst economic downturn in decades. I am more optimistic this time, or maybe I'm just getting accustomed to having a career in flux. I am encouraged in part because I have these avenues of expression: this book and the hope that it will encourage others, my blog at OneAmericanWriter.com, and new friends who are in various stages of job searches and business start-ups.

While I am still searching for a "permanent" position, I am taking an online course in online marketing and writing freelance articles for a small-town newspaper. Wish me well! I sincerely wish *you* well.

Read on! A few pages from now, I want to introduce you to two men who generously offered to share their experience and expertise with you.

Let's Get Started

These workbook pages provide the place to write down the action steps that can help you earn the money you need to survive and thrive until you find another career or another position in your field.

If you are between jobs but you are receiving unemployment or severance pay from your previous job, it might be a good idea to take these workbook steps now instead of waiting until that temporary source of income runs out. Perhaps you can provide a needed service in the community as a volunteer until you need to earn some income from your efforts.

If you are receiving unemployment benefits, be sure to report any income you earn, as required by each state. In North Carolina where I live, you can earn a certain amount of income before it starts reducing the benefit you receive from the government. Please try not to let unemployment benefits become a disincentive to work. The chance to make your own way is worth every effort.

Keep in mind that this book does not offer legal advice. You should seek professional advice and discuss income goals with family members, and always be guided by wisdom.

What a great chance to get to know some neighbors while you discover the service at which you have the most skill, and that you most enjoy providing, whether that is mowing lawns for elderly neighbors or offering software consulting or computer repair services to local families and small businesses.

In-box

From: Big Bad Boss
To: You
Subject: Which Direction?

Get up, get up, get up, get up, get up!
Don't just wake up like on other days. Get up
higher. Lift your head higher today, look up at
the sky more often today.

Plan a more glorious future for yourself today.
Why not? We only get one life. Make a bigger
plan, a more giving plan. Give more to your
goal, more to your neighbors, more to yourself in
the form of good things like rest and good
health...good habits that make your life richer
and more enjoyable.

Today is a good day to start getting up higher
than you are used to getting. GET UP!

Chapter 2: **Realize You Can**

If you don't think you can succeed, you probably won't. Let me make that more personal. If *I* don't think I can succeed, *I* won't. I was surprised to discover that the confidence I have in the workplace doesn't translate to my entrepreneurial efforts. Going it alone is scary. I think I forgot to pack my self-assurance in my cardboard box when I got laid off!

I remember, as a teen, sitting on the steps of the recreation center in off-base housing in Hampton, Virginia and hearing two of the in-crowd girls say they were afraid to sit near Rick as he sang and played his guitar. "What if he thinks we're losers?" one of them asked.

My friend and I were shocked to learn that these two "cool" girls were nervous about *anything*. We assumed they were filled with confidence to match their hair-tossing, hip-throwing swaggers. It boosted my own confidence to learn that even *they* were sometimes scared.

As we read about local and national success stories, we might assume that the men and women who are making it on their own had an idea and forged ahead fearlessly. In some cases, perhaps that is true.

A blogger recently posted: "Work like you're scared, but don't *be* scared." The author, Mark Riffey, writing for Flathead Beacon out of Flathead Valley, Montana, was referring to new tax laws scaring would-be business owners, but his advice applies more broadly.

I will twist his advice based on my own experience. Work *even though* you are scared. Work *with* your fear. Work *through* your fear. (This applies to job-searching, interviewing, *and* working for yourself.)

Allow me to quote my own recent blog post on this topic, titled, "My Fellow Chickens" at OneAmericanWriter.com.

My Fellow Chickens,

Like water washing over my parched nervous system, I read these words moments ago. "He rewrote pieces twenty times or more and sometimes pleaded with the postmaster of North Brooklin, Maine, to return a just-mailed manuscript so he could punch up its ending or rewrite the lead.

"In addition to being a consummate rewriter, White was a gifted procrastinator." E. B. White, of course. Woo hoo! I already know I'm not alone in my fear, but it feels SO GOOD to know I am in such good company.

And you? How chicken are you? This might help.

A recent post from copyblogger (see CopyBlogger.com), "5 Reasons Why Trying to Be Successful Will Keep You Poor," is really about fear, too, and overcoming it.

I especially like this from #5 in his post: "If success is achieved by taking repeated, meaningful action, then what happens if you're not confident enough to take the actions that scare the crap out of you?"

YEAH. The message I took away from this is RELAX INTO IT. You can't do it (write, publish, start a business) to be successful. You have to do it because it is meaningful to you.

And DON'T LET FEAR STOP YOU.

The E.B. White quote above is from a book I serendipitously found in a used bookstore today, "The Courage to Write; How Writers Transcend Fear" by Ralph Keyes. I can't wait to read the rest of the book to find out!

Mr. White is further quoted as considering himself, "....the second most inactive writer living, and the third most discouraged."

Let's be BRAVE, shall we? If he did it, we can do it. Good. Now, I'm going to bed. I'll be brave in the morning.

Ggggood Night,
Donna, One American Writer

Once you acknowledge that you *are* afraid in some respect, and that everyone you see deals with anxieties, start to identify and eliminate or counteract as many causes of anxiety as you can.

Obviously, you can't start a home-based business if you don't know how long you'll be in your current home. Even if you know you can pay the rent or mortgage for a full year without extra income, the potential need to downsize is unnerving if you don't have a plan. So before you start a money-making enterprise, do a quick inventory of your intentions so you know where you stand, and have a plan-B ready in case you need it.

If you have more house than you need, and you are still paying a mortgage, then you know you can make X number of mortgage payments before your savings and/or retirement money is gone. If you downsize *now*, assuming you can sell your home, you can afford your smaller home for a longer period of time, perhaps with a smaller income.

As Dave Ramsey, host of a financial ("Yell it with me, I'M DEBT FREE!") radio show often says, if you have been laid off, you are in emergency mode. Be sure to prioritize so you are on solid emotional ground before you start a business.

This workbook is designed to help you start on a shoestring. *Don't* spend money you can't afford to lose. *Don't* spend money on business cards and *then* find that you can't work up the nerve to market yourself. Start small using the steps in this book, earn some income, and *then* move forward – perhaps go back through these steps again with a more ambitious goal.

Another challenge is weeding through all of the junky information you find when researching home-business opportunities. How do you find the real information? How do you know which efforts work and which are scams?

For instance, a former neighbor works from home transcribing medical notes for doctors' offices. But when you research that field, you will find companies and individuals pedaling information you don't need. Some bloggers may offer solid information in exchange for your e-mail address, but beware of offers that charge you a fee. A solid place to start is by finding the association that serves that industry.

Check out IveTriedThat.com (slogan, "We lose money so you don't have to") to learn more about legitimate and bogus offers. I read about that site recently and I'm very glad someone is (I hope) earning some income by helping us save ours.

Got Insecurity?
Part of the reason you are reading *this* book is that *I* am reading a new book by Beth Moore titled, "So Long Insecurity; you've been a bad friend to us." Moore is a Bible teacher, but even if you don't agree with the book's Biblical foundation, the revelations of others' fears make readers feel more normal for having their own; this reader in particular. (And there is great insight into men's anxieties, too.) See SoLongInsecurity.com.

I am developing a workshop titled, "The Courage to Write, and Publish," based on Keyes' book. I dare *you* to work toward making your dream a reality. Once you know you are *not* alone in your fear, and you realize that *all* of the people who have businesses have fears and quirks, too, just like you, *then* you know *you can succeed*.

Working for yourself is not that big a deal. We worship entrepreneurs to such an extent that it makes us think becoming one is unattainable. Just be yourself, and start working. But first, *plan*.

Here's a quick exercise.

If you could choose two of the assets listed below to help you succeed, which would you choose?

- Rich relatives
- A brilliant mind
- Knowing the "right" people
- A beautiful face and physique
- A higher level of education or a degree in a different field
- Lots of free time
- A great new product idea

Whether we are talking about finding that next job, changing career fields, or making money from home, the following statement is true. Any of the above assets *without* action would get you *nowhere*. On the other hand, well-planned action, even without *any* of these assets, can bring you success. Use the tools provided in this workbook to create a solid plan of action. The networking I did to market my writing service gave me much more confidence for the long-haul job search, and taking the steps in this workbook can do the same for you.

Strip Off the Mystique

If you have ever worked from home or worked for yourself, you already know that it is not all it's cracked up to be. It is much easier and in many ways more fun to work for someone else, letting them take care of the paperwork, insurance, and taxes while you mingle with coworkers during breaks. Having said that, there are rewards for being self-employed that can never be achieved working for someone else. I will simply ask you to remember that working for yourself will demand some very, very hard work from you, the boss.

One Last Thing

Before you get started, if your house or apartment is a mess (don't worry; I'm not looking), I want to introduce you to FlyLady. She will help you get things straight, bit by bit, so that you can accomplish your job-seeking and moneymaking goals. She will encourage you every step of the way. (You'll never guess why I know this.)

Go to FlyLady.net and click "Getting Started" to sign up for her free e-mail group, or buy her book, *Sink Reflections*, by Marla Cilley (the FlyLady), available at FlyLady.net, Amazon.com, and Borders bookstores. Then take baby steps!

And Now, a Word from a Coworker

Before you decide which service to provide, I want you to know you are in good company as you deal with the impact of job loss.

Allow me to introduce Chuck Lehning, a talented writer and author. My children and I are enjoying the adventures of Sharlie and her team in "On Dragon's Wings," his novel, available at Lulu.com. Sharlie is Captain of the Guard in the town of Six Forks ... but you will have to read it yourself and I highly recommend it.

Chuck was very kind to write about his own experience being laid off several months before I was. His honesty as he talks about this kick in the gut has helped *me*, and I know it will help and encourage you, too. (I hope you will share this information with others you might know who are between jobs.)

Then, read an exclusive interview from an online publishing and marketing professional before you decide which product or service to provide in your own home-based business.

Chapter 3: **Chuck's Mistakes and Some Great Advice**

[Chuck Lehning] It came as a surprise to me. I could feel the gloom in the air when I walked into the office that morning. As soon as I got to my desk, the whole engineering group was called into a big meeting. That's never a good sign.

We were supposed to have at least another year before the large corporation that gobbled up our product phased it out. But the powers that be decided to rush the transition, thinking they would save money by laying off most of the people in our local office.

Less than five years ago I had taken a job with a small company. That company was bought by a larger company, which in turn was bought by a corporate giant. I guess they thought they were big enough that they did not care about the customers they would lose from canceling our product. But that wasn't my problem anymore. My problem was I was out of a job.

One would think I would have learned how to handle this situation by now. This was the third time I had been laid off. Alas, I began falling right back into the same unhealthy behavior patterns that I did the last two times I got laid off.

This time, however, I was able to look back and recognize those patterns. I can now see what I had done wrong in the past. Therefore, I'd like to share my mistakes to help others recognize and avoid these traps.

A Little Perspective

Before I go any further, I should tell you a little bit about myself, so you can see where I'm coming from. I am a Software Engineer – a fancy term for Computer Programmer. My career choice reveals a lot about my personality. I am a dispassionate, logical thinker. I am an introvert, not a people person. I'd rather visit the dentist than dial a telephone.

I don't respond well to rah-rah speeches. For heaven's sake, please don't tell me that my unemployment is an opportunity instead of a problem. I have bills to pay and no income! That is a PROBLEM!

I am not a good salesman. That includes not being able to sell myself. My lack of salesmanship makes it harder for me to land a job or start a business.

Networking is especially difficult for me. I hate hearing that 80% of all jobs landed nowadays are landed though networking. If I had good people skills, I wouldn't have become a programmer.

As I discuss my mistakes, I hope you will be able to see how my personality type has affected my decisions. Being laid off is a hard blow to anyone, regardless of personality type. For introverted types like me, unemployment can be even more stressful, because whether you intend to find a job or start a business, you must put yourself in front of other people to succeed.

Introverted or not, we are all human. Sudden unemployment will stress anyone. How we react to this painful circumstance will affect our happiness, our home life, our health and even our prospects of finding a new employment or business situation. Don't make the same mistakes I did.

Mistake Number 1: Panic

To misquote Woody from Toy Story, it seemed like the perfect time to panic to me. I was out of a job, and the economy was in the worst recession since World War II. The last time I had been laid off it took me over a year to find a job, and the economy wasn't in such bad shape then. Unlike last time, my wife was no longer working, meaning that we had no income other than unemployment.

Because of the state of the economy, I was afraid it would take me even longer than last time to find a job. I was afraid we would run out of money before I could find a job. Naturally, I felt panic rising within me. Although I'm normally a dispassionate and logical person, my situation looked so bad to me that the rising panic threatened to overwhelm my normally cold logic.

The problem with panic is that it makes you do things that may not be in your best interest. It can cause you to act impulsively, without fully thinking through the consequences.

For example, my panic caused me to immediately dive into a full-fledged job search. That was a mistake on my part. Before beginning my job search in earnest I should have taken some time to do the following.

Evaluate my career direction
Anyone in this position should take some time to review his or her life and career. Am I doing what I really want to be doing? Is it time to change my career direction or move into a new field? Do I want to work for someone else, or do I want to start my own business? Questions such as these should be answered *before* beginning a job search, because you don't want to let panic goad you into taking a direction that you really don't want to take.

Prepare for the job search
Preparing for a job search is a topic large enough for its own book, so I won't go into details here. Let's just say that there are several activities you need to spend time on before you will be ready for the search. For example, you will need to prepare a good resume and elevator speech. You will need to build your network. You will need to research companies you wish to target. You will need to practice interviewing techniques. Don't let panic goad you into beginning a job search you are not ready for. You will have a *much* better chance of landing a job if you are properly prepared.

Set aside some time for a low cost vacation

What? Vacation? I am *unemployed*; I don't need a vacation. It's ironic that when we're working, we have the money but not the time for vacation, and when unemployed we have the time but not the money. I believe that if you don't take some time off to just enjoy yourself before you begin your job search or start a business, you will regret it later. Searching for a job is a full-time job. You will not want to be away from home when scheduling interviews or waiting to hear back from companies. Don't let panic rob you of a chance to relax and enjoy some time off.

Another way that panic led me to act contrary to my own best interest was that I began applying for jobs that I really didn't want. When I heard that Company X was hiring, I immediately went to that company's Web site and started applying for jobs. Unfortunately, none of the jobs were in the area where I lived.

Landing one of those jobs would have forced me to relocate. I had only applied to jobs in areas I thought I might like to live, but a little research showed me that one of the jobs was in an area I wouldn't like after all. Of course, that was the only job to which I got a response. I found myself worried that I would be offered a job in an area where I didn't want to live. Ultimately, I was not offered the job, but I had let panic push me into a position I did not want to be in.

Panic can be difficult to fight. When you feel the urgency brought on by panic, you must be careful. Before you act, always ask yourself if you are acting impulsively. Have you thoroughly thought out the situation? Are you prepared? Have you done the necessary research? Don't let panic goad you into doing something you really don't want to do.

Mistake Number 2: Fear Paralysis

Although you should not let panic cause you to act too quickly, you must also guard against being paralyzed into taking no action at all.

Applying for programming jobs was within my comfort zone. But the easy way is not always the *best* way. Working as a programmer was good, but I had other aspirations. I had dreams of being an author; I had even written a novel. I also wanted to start a business.

So what did I do in pursuit of these goals? Well, nothing. Of course I didn't write well enough to *market* my own books. I'm no salesman, so of course I didn't have what it takes to start a business. At least those were the excuses I made.

Those excuses just served to cover up fears I had: fear of failure and fear of rejection. The fears were subtle. I did not directly recognize that I was afraid of pursuing my dreams. Instead, I used excuses to thwart any attempt to work toward those goals.

Here's how it works. I want to be an author. I wrote a novel. The next step would be to try to get the novel published. Now, I didn't sit down and say, "I fear rejection, so I won't submit my novel, because if I do it may be rejected." Instead, I said, "The market is very competitive. Very few aspiring authors are able to get their books published. Trying to get this book published will be a waste of time and money." See how logical that sounds?

Let me be clear about this fear of rejection. Most people have some fear of rejection. The fear itself is not the problem. The problem is that it can influence your decision making, especially if you aren't consciously aware of its presence.

Nor am I saying that you should boldly go where logic says not to go. I know I can't sing. There is nothing wrong with honestly admitting that I couldn't carry a tune in a bucket. If I had the dream of becoming the next country-music star, it really would be foolish for me to pursue it, because I just don't have the talent for that, and I never will.

Writing is a different story for me. I do have at least some writing skills. I've been told this be teachers, bosses and coworkers. Do I have the talent to become a novelist? Maybe. Maybe not. But I won't ever know, unless I try. The honestly logical thing for me to do would be to submit my writing to criticism. I could, for example, join a writers' club and allow other writers to review my work. Not only would I find out if I have the potential, but I could learn how to improve my skills. Maybe I don't yet have what it takes, but perhaps I could develop the talent.

It is possible that acting to pursue my dream to become a novelist will result in rejection and ultimately failure. However, if I make excuses in order to cover my fear of rejection, I will guarantee my failure.

I also let fear of failure influence me into making excuses for not starting a business of my own. The scenario was similar to my novel-writing dream. Rather than using research and sound thinking to guide my decisions, I made up a series of excuses which allowed me to take no action.

I cannot deny that starting a business does carry some amount of risk. Often there are significant amounts of money at risk. Having a major part of your savings at risk is a frightening prospect for most people, as it should be. I am not saying that the fear of failure associated with risk should be ignored. It is there to tell you, "Hey, you need to think this through!"

My problem was that rather than giving the project the honest, critical thought it deserved, I just told myself, "It's just too risky. I can't raise the capital I need. It's just not going to work."

Did I do any market research to see if my business idea was workable? Well, no. Did I survey people to determine what they would pay for my product? Uh, no. Did I write a business plan? Did I look for sources of capital? Did I contact the SBA or SCORE (Small Business Administration or Senior Core of Retired Executives)? No, no and no. So did I really know that my business idea would fail? Of course not!

I'm not saying that you should act rashly or act without thinking. I'm saying that you shouldn't allow yourself to *not* act without really thinking it through. There is a lot of work you must do before you can honestly determine whether or not a business idea is viable. Don't allow yourself to make excuses to *not* act before doing the necessary research and putting in the required effort. If you do, you will be letting fear make your decisions for you.

Mistake Number 3: Wasting Time

"Don't waste time," is an axiom that should be, and probably is, obvious to most of us. The only reason I feel the need to mention it is that it is such an *easy* trap to fall into.

When I look back at my life, I am amazed at the sheer amount of time that I have wasted, time that can never be reclaimed. Admittedly, not everyone is as bad as I am when it comes to wasting time. I find that I need to be constantly on guard to avoid wasting time. There are so many things that vie for my attention: the television, video games, the Internet, even books.

When the task I'm working on is tedious or just not fun, I feel myself drawn to one of my favorite time-wasting activities. It's just so easy to turn that TV on or start up that video game. Let's face it; we all like to be entertained. We all prefer doing something enjoyable to something that feels like work.

My most serious weakness is video games. Yes I am a geek. Like many people I tend to have some attention-deficit issues, and it's amazing how a good video game can help me focus. All the troubles and concerns that create stress in my life just melt away as I build an army to overrun the opponent's base. Completing a level or defeating a boss fills me with a sense of accomplishment. Playing video games just makes me feel good. It is very much like a drug, and like any other drug, it is addictive and subject to abuse.

The same can be said of any other time-wasting activity. Do you use TV to make you feel better or forget your troubles? If so, it's a drug. I know that statement may sound overly serious, but even an activity as benign as reading books can be detrimental to your wellbeing if abused. If for no other reason, it is serious because *you need that time* for more productive activities!

A job search is a full-time job. You've got to write a resume, research companies, network, etc. Starting a business is also a *lot* of work. You've got market research to do, a business plan to write, legal filings, equipment purchases, and so on. You can't afford to spend your time playing video games

Previously, I said that it may be a good idea to take some time off to enjoy yourself prior to beginning your job search or starting a business. However, once you begin your job search or the process of starting a business, you should start paying careful attention to the way you spend your time.

So how can someone avoid wasting so much time? Perhaps one of the simplest things to do is to set aside time for productive activities. Before you were laid off, you worked for eight hours (at least) per weekday. Even though you are not working now, you should still set aside a similar amount of time each day. Consider this time to be your work time. Just having this simple boundary in place can help you keep your time productive. You wouldn't watch TV at work, so don't do it during your work time. Remember that this time is set aside to work for *you*.

Your work time does not need to be lumped into one solid eight-hour block. You could break it down into smaller chunks with some designated off-time inserted between the chunks. Do something refreshing or fun during these off-times, but be sure that you get back to work on time. A task-oriented person may want to break his or her work down into easily managed tasks and then insert some off-time between tasks. But remember to get back to work when the designated off-time is over. A regular work schedule will help you keep your work time productive.

Like many people, I have difficulty concentrating on the task at hand when it's quiet. I like to have some kind of background noise when I work.

If you are like this, then having some background music or the radio -- not talk radio – on is okay during your work time. The television, however, is *not* an acceptable source of background noise. It is far too distracting.

Sometimes more drastic measures are needed to keep distracting activities from wasting your time. Cancel your cable or satellite TV. You will remove a temptation and save some money at the same time. Put away the game console and uninstall the games from your computer. Put your game discs somewhere difficult to access, like in a box in the back of a closet. Lend them to a neighbor, or have a family member hide them from you. The harder they are to get to, the less of a temptation they will be.

Believe me. I understand the need to just veg-out sometimes. But the key word here is "sometimes." There were plenty of times when I would get home from work and feel so spent that I couldn't focus on anything productive. But once I was laid off, I no longer had that excuse! It's okay to set aside a little time to play, but first make sure that you have satisfied your work-time quota.

Ultimately, you want to make sure that your time is spent productively. You want to be able to look at what you are doing at any given moment and determine if that activity is productive or wasteful. What do I mean by productive? I mean that this activity is helping you reach your goals.

Here are some questions to ask to determine if an activity is productive:
- Is this helping me land a job?
- Is this making me more desirable to a prospective employer?
- Is this helping me define my career path?
- Is this helping me start my business?
- Is this helping me determine if my business idea is viable?
- Is this educating me? (No, watching "Mythbusters" is *not*).
- Is this helping me improve my skills?
- Is this helping my family?
- Is this helping others?

Some activities that can lead to wasting time may have appropriate uses. For example, the Internet may have already displaced television as the number one devourer of hours. Yet, the Internet is also a vital job-hunting tool. Use the Internet for productive activities, but be careful. I remember a time when I was conducting online research into medieval naval warfare tactics for a book I was writing. This was a perfectly valid and productive activity. However, as one hyperlink lead to another, I eventually found myself looking at a list of 1960's cartoons. Somewhere, I had gone from being productive to wasting time.

Like time spent on any other activity, time spent on hobbies should also be evaluated. Some hobbies can be productive. Indeed, hobbies can sometimes lead to a new career path. Perhaps your love of cooking will lead you to open a catering business. There are other ways hobbies can be productive. A lover of woodworking may find many ways to improve his house. Perhaps he can make Christmas gifts for friends rather than buying them. A computer programmer can help out with an open-source project, helping others and improving his skill-set at the same time.

Some hobbies, like stamp collecting, are just for fun. Others may help you improve yourself. Some, like painting or dancing, give you the opportunity to be creative and express yourself. Others, like running or swimming, may help you stay in shape or lose weight. In general, I don't consider time spent on hobbies to be wasted. However, even the most productive of hobbies should not be allowed to encroach on the work time you have set aside. Unless you are directly converting the hobby into a business or job opportunity, time spent on the hobby should be relegated to play time.

Mistake Number 4: Getting Down on Yourself

When unemployed, it is so *very* easy to get down on yourself. This is a dangerous mistake. While addressing this subject, I will try to avoid spouting platitudes and psycho-babble. They roll of the tongue easily, but they don't help. I cannot overstress the importance of avoiding this trap. It is the fastest way to nowhere.

If you allow yourself to beat yourself up, if you allow yourself to harbor feelings of worthlessness and uselessness, if you allow yourself to fall into depression, then you can truly damage your chances of landing a job or starting a business. Do not allow this to happen!

For me personally, this is the most difficult trap to avoid. I tend to be both a pessimist and a perfectionist. I am harder on myself than anyone else. If you, too, are like this, that doesn't mean you are psychologically flawed. Indeed, you are in good company. However, it does mean that you are vulnerable to the trap of getting down on yourself.

When someone says to you, "Tell me about yourself," do you begin your answer by describing what you do for a living? We tend to identify ourselves with our jobs. Men especially tend to derive a large portion of their significance from their jobs. So it's easy to see how being unemployed can damage a person's view of their own worth. If job equals worth, then no job equals no worth.

People want to be independent. We respect independence. We want to be able to provide for ourselves and our families. If we can't do that because of a job loss, then we have less respect for ourselves. *This is not a psychological flaw!* The fact that we are designed this way encourages us to be providers and productive members of society.

While the association of work and worth provides good motivation, we must recognize that work and worth are *not* the same. Your job is not your worth. At the risk of sounding like I am throwing out platitudes, let me say this again. *Your job is not your worth!* Your overall value as a person does not rest in the work you get paid to do. There are many other ways that we, as people, add value to the world around us. Even something as simple as loving your family is more valuable to the world as a whole than anything you will ever get paid to do. Sometimes we have to remind ourselves of this when the weight of unemployment is pushing us down.

Remember also that being unemployed is a temporary state. This short phase of your life is not big enough to define your whole life.

In addition to unemployment itself, the process of the job search can be very discouraging. The emotional rollercoaster is appropriate symbolism for the job search. Getting an interview or making it to the next step can be a high. The anticipation of waiting for a response can be excruciating. Not getting a job you had high hopes for can be devastating. Being turned down for job after job will grind you down.

My last bout with unemployment lasted over a year. Many job opportunities appeared and then floated away just outside of my grasp. I was an experienced software engineer. I held college degrees in computer science and aerospace engineering. Yet I was unable to even get a job as a cashier in a retail store. (It can be difficult to get a job for which you are over-qualified. Managers are afraid you will find a better job and leave.)

Needless to say I was pretty discouraged. I began to ask myself, "Am I so useless that no one will hire me?" I don't like feeling useless any more than the next person, so I was really getting down on myself.

What I didn't realize was that not being able to market my skills into a job was not the same as being useless. There are many reasons you can be turned down for a job, especially when there is a lot of competition for jobs. A company can be very choosey when looking for the best fit for the position.

Perhaps my skill set wasn't the absolute best fit for the position. Perhaps I made mistakes on my programming test. Perhaps I misspelled the interviewer's name in my thank-you note. Maybe they just didn't like the way I looked or talked. None of these things meant I was useless. There were a lot of other useful people who got turned down for the same jobs I did.

Remember also that your usefulness is not defined solely by your job skills. We all have skills and abilities that we use to help those around us, even if we are not currently using them to earn money. Do you read to your children? Do you sing in the choir at church? Do you help your parents with their computer issues? Do you help your friends move? Do you mow your grass? Do you help your landlady carry out her garbage? These things may be small but they contribute greatly to our overall usefulness as a person.

I have stressed the importance of recognizing and refuting feelings of worthlessness and uselessness because they can lead to depression. I am not a psychologist, so I cannot offer advice for dealing with depression once it sets in. If you already have fallen into depression, please seek help. Depression is not where you want to be. It will paralyze you and severely impact your job search.

Other than being aware of their existence and the reasons they are not true, are there any practical actions I can take to avoid feelings of worthlessness and uselessness? Yes! I believe that the most effective way to avoid those feelings is to volunteer. Volunteering helps you maintain your sense of worth and usefulness even more than holding a regular job.

There are many places you can volunteer. So many charitable organizations and churches need help. You should be able to find one that supports a cause you care about. Do you want to help the homeless? Do you want to help homeless animals? Do want to teach Sunday school? Would you like to deliver meals to shut-ins? I cannot list all the organizations that would love the opportunity to make you feel useful.

Often, specialized skills such as medical or computer skills are in great demand by these organizations. If you have skills like these, you are needed terribly. Even with limited skills, just a willingness to help will make you valuable. Other opportunities to volunteer can be found at large events like a Special Olympics meet or a local arts festival. Sometimes small businesses will allow you to do volunteer work for them. This can be a great way to become acquainted with the field. Find a small business in your field of interest and ask about volunteering.

As I said, volunteering will help you maintain your sense of self-worth. It gives you something to point to and honestly say, "Here, I am valuable. I am useful. I am needed." Not only does it feel good to volunteer, but it also adds real value to the world you live in.

While I was working at a software company developing internet ad-serving software, my wife worked in several volunteer positions. She helped at a cat-adoption organization. She helped teach an ESL (English as a second language) class. She also worked at an organization that helps prevent people from becoming homeless. Which of us do you think added more value to the world around us?

Volunteering can have other benefits, too.
- Depending on the work you do, you may be able to add to your skill set or improve skills you already have.
- Volunteering looks good on a resume. You can add skills you use to your resume.
- Volunteering provides opportunities for networking. You will meet new people. Who knows? Some of those people might be or know key people in your field.

Even after you land a job or start a business, I recommend volunteering when you can. Its benefits do not go way once you start working again.

Chuck will share one more mistake with us in a later chapter. Meanwhile, as you plan your home-based effort, and perhaps also continue your job search, let's hear what Chuck has to say about your financial future.

Chapter 4: **Avoid the Piggy Bank Blues**

[Chuck Lehning] Years ago it was common to work for a single company for your entire career. Nowadays, the job market seems to have taken on a much more cyclic nature. People tend to work for one place for a while and then move on to somewhere else. That's not the way I would like it to be, but that's the reality we have to deal with. The odds are that your next job will not last for the rest of your career. You will likely face job loss again. I think it's a good idea to be prepared for that job loss when it does occur. (I did not title this section "Mistake Number Six" because preparing myself financially was one thing I did right.)

Obviously, one of the most stressful aspects of job loss is the impact on your finances. This stress can be greatly reduced by keeping yourself on sound financial ground while you still have that paycheck. If you are living paycheck to paycheck, a sudden job loss will immediately put you in financial trouble, causing you and your family undue stress and limiting your options.

The plan for financial stability is actually very simple, but unfortunately it can be difficult to carry out. Here is the plan in its entirety: 1. Stay out of debt. 2. Save money.

See, I told you it was simple. The problem is that most Americans tend to live a more expensive lifestyle than they can afford. This leads us to the third, but perhaps most important, step in the plan: 3. *Evaluate your lifestyle*.

First, stay out of debt. With the possible exception of your home mortgage, you should have no other debt whatsoever. NONE! This means no credit-card debt, no car loan, no boat loan and no home improvement loan.

You should never carry a balance on your credit cards; pay them off *every month*. Before you purchase an item with a credit card, stop to think about it. *If you don't have the money in the bank to cover that purchase, then you can't afford it!* Always keep track of how much you have charged on your credit cards, so that you don't run the risk of exceeding the amount of money you can afford to spend.

Yes, I did say no car loan. So what if you're an executive pulling down a hundred grand a year. That doesn't entitle you to drive a Lexus. *If you don't have the money in the bank to pay for the car with cash, then you can't afford it!* Those of us with more modest incomes may need to look at used cars. We may have to settle for a smaller, less sporty, less luxurious car than we would like.

This same attitude must be taken with any purchase, be it furniture, a computer, or a really big TV. If you don't have the money on hand right now, then you cannot afford it. The only exception that I make to this rule is a house. You have to live somewhere. If you don't own a home, then you will be paying rent. For some people it makes more sense to be paying on a mortgage and building equity in the home than it does to be paying rent. Of course any potential homebuyer should have a good down payment. I don't care how great a deal the bank tries to give you. Financing more than 80% of your home is financial lunacy.

Second, save money. I'm not talking about shopping for bargains or clipping coupons – although these practices will help. I'm talking about putting away money for the future. Few people save as much as they should. You should think of saving as paying yourself. Indeed, when you save you *are* paying for your future.

Naturally, you should be putting money away for retirement. You have been contributing to a 401K or IRA, haven't you? Even though this money will not be readily available to you during your next job loss, it is vitally important that you put away what you can for retirement while you are working. You won't be able to do much retirement saving when you are unemployed.

To properly prepare for your next job loss, you must additionally stash some cash in some kind of readily accessible savings account. This is the money you will tap into to carry you through your unemployment. Make sure the money is in a place where you will be able to get to it when you need it. Some experts say you should have at least three months of salary set aside. As someone who was out of work for a year, I would recommend more, perhaps six months.

I am not qualified to give advice on where you should put either your retirement or job-loss savings. Each person's unique situation demands individual solutions. My advice is just that you *do* save. You will thank yourself later.

Third, evaluate your lifestyle. As I said before, the main reason Americans have trouble saving and staying out of debt is that they try to live a lifestyle they can't afford. People have more house than they can afford, more car than they can afford, just more stuff in general than they can afford. It's an easy trap to fall into. Credit (i.e. debt) is so easy to come by. And with everyone else around you doing it too, you find yourself saying, "I should be able to afford that."

Okay, that's enough preaching. My aim is not to be judgmental of your lifestyle. My aim is to encourage *you* to judge your lifestyle. If you're not having any problem staying out of debt and saving at the same time, then you're all set. If you are, you may want to look at where your money goes.

You know the drill. Create a budget and track *everything* you spend. You may be surprised at where the money goes. Separate the things you need to spend money on (food, medicine, rent) from the things you don't (TV, Wiis, iPhones). Look for where you can make cuts. Perhaps the house or car can be downsized.

There is no shame in downsizing. There is no shame in living below your means. Some people may even see it as a sign of intelligence. It all boils down to making choices. It's up to you to decide if downsizing is what you must do to be financially prepared for the next job loss. Once you start working again or get established in your new business, I encourage you to start right away preparing yourself financially for the next job loss. Consider your options while you still have choices to make.

After taking Chuck's advice to heart, I invite you to read my exclusive interview with Peter A. Prestipino, Editor in Chief at Website Magazine (WebsiteMagazine.com and the monthly print edition). He knows what it takes to make money online, and his encouragement motivates me every time I read his answers below.

Chapter 5: **Make Money Online? Exclusive Interview**

I have read the print and online editions of Website Magazine over the years and I find it to be one of the most authoritative and useful resources available. I contacted their staff via e-mail, and Editor in Chief Peter A. Prestipino generously agreed to a phone interview for this book.

I spoke with Mr. Prestipino in June of 2009, a few months after Chuck was laid off, and six months before *I* was laid off again. His words continue to encourage me even as I include our conversation here.

Q. Website Magazine offers so much information for businesses that want to market online, but what would you say to the person sitting at home who keeps hearing about making money with a Web site?

A. As in all things, there are no shortcuts in life. You should do the best you can to educate yourself. You can go the route of doing all of the work yourself, or you can outsource and pay someone to do a lot of the work.

If you don't know what that service provider is talking about, you can take a wrong path and waste a lot of money. When you have educated yourself, you make better informed decisions that will benefit your business.

Q. In addition to Website Magazine (the print and online version), is there one book that you recommend people read?

A. There are so many – there are a lot of little books on search engine optimization (SEO), on design and marketing. When we have new staff here, it can take six months to get up to speed.

Set reasonable expectations. My sister makes baby blankets and she asks me, "How can I make more money?" Well, it relates to what you're already doing. If you are a plumber, or you have a golf course, or you work internationally printing business cards, you create a formal plan. It starts with being knowledgeable about what you already do.

Q. Where can people go when they first visit WebsiteMagazine.com to learn the step-by-step actions they need to take?

A. Our managing editor is creating those guides right now. She is providing direction such as, the first thing to look at is your URL. What is that, how do you get it, what are your options? Then, you consider hosting. Do you use open source or use a hosting provider? Then there's marketing…SEO and then maybe paid advertising, and then design. And of course, content is key from the beginning – providing content based on your expertise.

Q. Many authors, for instance, are told by their publishers to "Get a Web site!" but they don't know what to do. What do you recommend?

A. Wordpress is sort of the default, easy-to-use option. It can be self-hosted or you can find someone to host it for you. Sitemasher is one of our advertisers but even if they weren't, I would say they offer an excellent service. Yola is another good option.

Q. What about making money from a Web site…site monetization?

A. I was speaking at AdTech in San Francisco in April and the entire hour-and-a-half discussion was around alternatives to AdSense (a program to display Google ads on a Web site). They were asking, "How do content publishers make money?" And the beauty of it is, there are so many ways.

For instance, there's Amazon EC2 (Elastic Compute Cloud, a developer platform). If you become an Amazon Associate, on your Web site you can say you found a great book on writing resumes. You provide the official description of the book, and a link for your Web-site readers to purchase it from Amazon.

People know they can make money selling things on eBay, but they may not know that eBay has a new partner program. Since I'm a little tech-savvy, I put up a site to try this out, and I got an XML feed from eBay, and I list products that I think people will be interested in. It's making money and I'm not doing anything. I'm just sitting around – I go home and see how much money I made. Not a lot – it's incremental.

I know people who don't have any technical knowledge who make good money, but they're doing it 12 hours a day. They're writing their content, they are reading others' content and commenting and linking back to their sites. They are vested.

Q. What more can you say about monetization?

A. Well there's content – e-books, like you're doing, and then there's the service model. If you have an area of expertise, you can have someone build you a piece of software and sell it. That's how people make money – not only by affiliates, but by selling their own service – *build* something.

You might take two years to build it, but you still make way more money. Say, "Let me leverage my own expertise."

What do people say? "Do what you love, and you add another day to your week." Follow your passion. If golf is your passion, why not write an e-book about the best golf courses? Or write an iPhone app – make a golf-course finder. You'll get some attention.

Q. What about some related advice for people who are job searching?

A. You position yourself. You remain in the industry! That's what will be attractive to a potential employer. Not, "I sat around on my couch all day – I sent out resumes," but, "I created this Web site. I have an interest in this field, Mr. Interviewer, and I created this related Web site and I have a lot of knowledge here."

Q. My advice to folks is that the most important thing is to stay encouraged. What is your primary advice to the people who have been cut out of the corporate world for now?

A. Be relentless. Never care what people think.

Someone will always say, "That's a bad idea," but you have to jump in there and swim. Life is a big, deep pool so you had better start swimming. If they're standing on the shore saying you're going to drown, well *they're* not in the water. Jump in and swim!

Of course be ethical and moral, and be relentless. *Never* be scared. Have a goal. Most people don't have goals. They have a goal to pay the mortgage, and that is a goal and then there's the mortgage the next month. That's not really a goal. Have a goal and work systematically toward it.

Q. I know some people who are planning on creating something, but I get the feeling they still feel like it's a pipe dream – like it will never really happen.

A. It *will* happen. Do what you're passionate about. Leverage your expertise, and it will happen. Have a goal and never be scared. It goes back to "there are no shortcuts."
--

The steps in this workbook talk a bit about using online resources, but I don't go into making money exclusively online. My favorite advice is to *act* locally and *think* globally. Build your business around your current expertise and when it's time to create your Web site, keep following the steps in this book and turn to Website Magazine (and subscribe to a few well-chosen marketing bloggers) for online resources.

Ready to get started? Got a pen or pencil handy? Let's go!

Chapter 6: **Decide which Service to Provide**

Here's a chance to work at what you love. What are you good at? If you are an artist, try displaying a few pieces at a flea market and accepting commissions to paint murals in homes or businesses. That method of face-to-face "advertising" might be less expensive and a lot more fun than placing a classified ad in the local paper. If you enjoy cooking, teach a few mouthwatering specialties to local folks who lack culinary know-how. Or perhaps you could provide tutoring services to help a few local students while earning an income.

If you want to provide a more basic service, such as after-school-care or house-cleaning, you might be surprised to find it can be more satisfying than working for an established business.

Whatever service you plan to provide, think about continuing to provide that service on the side after you find a job. The freelance articles I had written while working at MCI were part of the reason I landed the position as a technical writer. Today, I write on my lunch hour. I may need that additional income to become my primary income source some day. And in your case, it might be wise to continue to provide a service as a sideline business when you find your next job.

After you decide on two or three services you might like to provide, you can conduct an informal survey to test the market. But first, a word about someone you probably know very well…your negative self.

Worrywart

Let's call the negative part of you a worrywart, courtesy of my Mom. My Mom is so in touch with her negative-self that once, daydreaming out loud to me and my sister, she said while doodling her dream house, "I would love to have a house with enough land to build a home nearby for you girls. Then it wouldn't be so far for the grandkids to come and visit … but

43

it would probably rain that day -" she caught herself, "Ooh – that's bad, isn't it?" She rained on her own daydream.

And yet she always encouraged us not to be "such a worrywart," which I just noticed is underlined in green when I type it hyphenated. Aha, it is an actual word according to my spell-check. Let's look it up. (I thought my Mom made it up.)

According to Dictionary.com, a worrywart is "One who worries excessively and needlessly," or someone who, "thinks about unfortunate things that might happen." Fuss-budget and fusspot are listed as synonyms. As we work through the remaining pages of this workbook, remember that the worrywart doesn't want to rain on your parade. It wants to cancel the parade on a sunny morning because it still *might* rain.

I like something my friend Stephanie shared with me recently. She read somewhere that you should schedule your worry time. That way, when a worry tries to interrupt your action-plan, you can just tell that worrywart part of you that you have a scheduled time to worry, and *this* is not it. If you need help in this area, why not set aside twenty minutes at 10 am to worry, and make a project out of it? If you sit there and try to worry, you might just see how funny it is, and chase those worries away. (Be sure to follow up the scheduled worry-time with a scheduled happy-thought time to get back on a positive track.)

Now, with your worrywart stuffed firmly in the closet, use the *Which Service Should I Provide* worksheet to help you discover the service you would most like to provide.

Worksheet: Which Service should I Provide?

Read this list and circle every service that lights a tiny spark in you. Don't let that internal negative voice stop you from circling whatever you want to circle.

Lawn care, craft lessons, shopping service, business writing, organizer, tour organizer, lunch cart, cleaning, training, child care, tutoring, birthday party entertainment, taxi service, computer help, answering service, personal coach (sports, exercise, or life planning), real-estate assistant, typing / word processing, research service, aerobics instructor, seamstress / alterations, career-change consultant, resume writer, music lessons, executive errand service, house or pet sitting, window washing, paper hanging, elder care, videotape events, bookkeeper, wedding planner, reupholster - or custom slipcovers, meeting / event planner, catering, grocery shopping and delivery service, babysitting (do you know how much babysitters earn today?).

Add your Own

Think of services local people pay for. Grab your local phone book or do a local search online for ideas. Identify local needs and add them here.

More Service Ideas:

CAUTION – Do *not* spend money you cannot afford to spend on any of these ideas. Please use wisdom. Earn the money first, *and then* invest in more supplies.

Local Service Survey

Once you have decided on a service to provide, or narrowed it down to a top-three list, conduct a survey to learn more about the market for your service. You might discover your first client with this survey, too.

Use these sample phrases or come up with your own survey questions.

Sample Phrases for your Survey

If I decided to provide a local service, which of the three listed here do you think I am most qualified to provide?

Which of the three do you think is most needed in our area?

If you use a local service provider for any of these three services, please tell me how you currently find a provider, and how satisfied you are with the service.

1. How did you find the service provider? Word-of-mouth, classified advertising, local business meeting, Internet?

2. What do you like most about the service you receive?

3. What do you wish they would do differently?

For the service you are most likely to need in the near future, what have you paid in the past and what is a fair rate to charge?

Use some of the questions above and some of your own on the following worksheet to build your own *Local Service Survey*.

Worksheet: Local Service Survey

Use the sample questions above to create your survey.

Service Option:	
Service Option:	
Service Option:	

Question	Answer

Optional

Name:
Phone and / or E-mail:

In-box

> **From:** Big Bad Boss
> **To:** You
> **Subject:** Get thee to a thrift store
>
> Purchase thou something for thy home office.
> I found a great wood filing cabinet with
> lock and keys for $10. What will *you* find?
>
> Then get back to your home office, ignore
> the toys on the floor (kids!) and WORK and
> WORK and WORK and WORK and WORK.
>
> Here's an acronym for you:
> **W** - Wonderful
>
> **O** - Opportunity to
>
> **R** - Reinvent your
>
> **K** - Krazy life

Chapter 7: **Set Up Your Home Office**

If you have not yet set up a workspace for your job search, you can take care of that now. Depending on your work style, you might want to use the same area for your job search *and* your service business, but it might be easier to stay organized if you keep those areas separate. I use one desk with the drawers on one side devoted to my freelance writing material while the drawers on the other side collect papers related to everything else in life.

Where will you work?

If you have a spare room, you can start with your own home office. Most of us, however, will have to be content with the corner of a room, or even the corner of a table. I have read about folks who used an old door across two filing cabinets as a desk, and others who converted a walk-in closet and a nook under the stairs into work areas.

You will quickly discover how your workspace impacts your working habits. When I got my first desk I could never seem to make myself sit at it. My favorite method was a "floating office." I used a wooden box and a portfolio (zippered notebook) that I took with me to whatever room the family was in, and I worked while they "familied."

I learned that my work area must be near all of the distractions of family life in order for me to work effectively. When I need to work without interruption, I get up long before the rest of the family awakes. I also take advantage of those few times when I can't sleep. If I wake up at 2 AM and can't get back to sleep (a hazard of starting a part-time home-based business…your mind races) I get up and write for a couple of hours and then get one or two more hours of sleep before my normal waking time.

Use the *Workspace Inventory* worksheet to help you determine the best current solution for your home-office workspace.

Example

- **Area** - Kitchen Nook

- **Plus** - Near phone; plenty of natural light; can hear phone and door; can keep an eye on cooking / laundry.

- **Minus** - Too near refrigerator traffic; no door to close for privacy; can hear TV in next room.

Worksheet: Workspace Inventory

Think creatively as you take inventory of your living area to see where you might create a workspace such as the kitchen nook (let the family eat in the dining room) or the corner by the bookshelf (use the shelves to hold supplies) or perhaps half of your bedroom.

Area	Plus	Minus

Remember to Shop Cheap!

Visit thrift shops, flea markets and yard sales for many of the items you will need. If you need to buy a used computer, I have found that a shop that sells used computers will help me when mine gives me trouble, whereas if I buy one listed in Craigslist by an individual, I would never expect help from that person later.

We once bought a used IBM ThinkPad laptop for $300 when our budget would have put a new laptop purchase into the next decade, and I found a small copy machine for $20 at a yard sale. The laptop worked well until we let the children play with it, and the copier still serves us well.

Reward, then Work

Once you've come this far, reward yourself in some small but tangible way. Have a quick simple celebration, like a meal prepared with special care and shared with family or a friend, or enjoyed by yourself with your favorite music playing. Or do a dance in the living room and whoop it up for a minute to two, watch your favorite funny movie (not a depressing drama), or take a walk down the street and savor the sky as you send up thanks for your progress so far.

Celebrating your small successes is very important. Establish this habit and take it with you into your future business or employment situation and watch the change in your attitude toward life. Practice this at home, too. When I taught stress management as part of a customer service course at MCI, I developed a simple concept I called, "Success after success after success." Acknowledge that, at the end of each day, unless you fell off the planet, your day was filled with many small successes, even on days when you made a few mistakes. Celebrate! OK, now *back to work.*

Celebrate success after success after success!

Now, before you create your action plan, let's hear from Chuck once more as he shares the fifth mistake he made when he was laid off. Then, be sure to gain the expertise you need as soon as you can.

Chapter 8: **Mistake – Going at It Alone**

[Chuck Lehning: "Mistake Number 5: Going It Alone"] I am an introvert, a loner by nature, so naturally I try to do everything on my own. This is, of course, a mistake, because, like it or not, we all need the help of others whether we are trying to land a job or start a business.

Most of us like the idea of being independent, of being able to provide for ourselves. The reality is that people are social creatures, who are as dependent on each other as ants are dependent on the colony.

Do you grow your own food? Do you fix your own car? Do you build your own computers? Do you generate your own electricity? Do you forge your own steel? Do you manufacture your own paper? Some people can answer yes to some of these questions, but I don't think anyone can answer yes to all of them. If you can't, then you are dependent on other people.

There is no shame in depending on others to do what you cannot do. Remember, others are also dependent, and some will depend on *you* to do want they cannot do for themselves. This is how civilization works.

There are several ways you will need to utilize other people. If you are searching for a job, one of the most important things you can do is develop a network. You need to make contacts that can lead you to a new job. I know that meeting strangers is difficult for a lot of people, myself included. But sometimes you just have to suck it up and assert your will over your feelings. The last time I was unemployed I did almost no networking. Maybe that's why it took me so long to find a job.

If you really struggle with meeting new people, perhaps you can make it easier on yourself by taking a more outgoing friend with you and networking together. Perhaps online networking sites will work better for you.

You should also utilize other people to examine your resume and cover letters. I once found a grammar mistake on a resume I had been using for months. Arrg! I wish I had let someone check that resume earlier. You also need to let people help you practice interviewing. In addition to friends and family, you could enlist the help of friends who have recently searched for a job or had the responsibility of hiring people. They will be up on the latest job-search and hiring techniques. They may even be able to help you with the format and content of your resume. Don't be afraid to ask!

If you are starting a business, you will need all kinds of help. For some things, you may be able to elicit the aid of friends and family. Don't be afraid to ask! For the more specialized services, like those of a lawyer or accountant, you may need to hire someone.

In any type of business, there are some aspects that are best understood by people already in that field. I highly recommend seeking the advice of someone already established in a business like yours. You might be surprised at how helpful they will be. Small-business owners usually like to see other small-business owners succeed. Don't be afraid to ask. (Do I sound like I'm repeating myself?)

You may also want to check out any professional organizations associated with your business field. In addition, be sure to check out the SBA and SCORE. They offer a lot of free help.

Here is a short list of the types of people you will need to utilize:
- **Lawyer**: There are several tasks for which you may need a business attorney – determining whether to be a sole proprietor or a corporation, registering your business, registering a trademark or patent, reviewing a lease or employment policies. Look for someone with small-business expertise.

- **Accountant**: In addition to bookkeeping, an accountant can help with tax issues and the paperwork necessary for hiring employees. Again, look for someone with small-business expertise.

- **Commercial Real Estate Agent**: If your business will involve a storefront, you may want the services of a commercial Realtor® to help you find the best location.

- **Computer Geek**: Most businesses nowadays rely on computers for tasks such as bookkeeping and inventory. Unless you are a computer guru, you will need help with equipment purchase and setup, software installation, networking, etc. If your business will have a Web site, you may need help with site hosting and creation.

- **Manual Labor**: Are you going to be moving equipment or inventory? Never underestimate the value of a friend with a truck.

- **Skilled Labor**: If you are going to be setting up a storefront, office or home office, you may need the help of a carpenter, electrician, plumber, etc.

- **Graphic Designer**: A graphic designer, whether a hired professional or an artistic friend, can help you design your logo, advertising materials, Web site, and signage.

- **Backup/Employees**: Will you have someone who can tend to the business when you are sick or on vacation? Or will you hire employees to help you run your business?

In addition, you don't want to disregard the value of having friends to provide moral support and accountability. Let's face it; being unemployed is a difficult and stressful time for anyone. The encouragement of friends is a valuable tool for keeping your spirits up, and high spirits increase your chance of success. There is no shame in needing the support of friends. It is the way our species is designed. Even the most introverted of us, such as myself, will find the encouragement of a friend or family member to be powerfully uplifting. Don't be afraid to discuss your concerns with a friend or family member.

The accountability provided by a friend will also be a valuable tool. It's one thing to say, "I'm going to do X." Then when X becomes difficult or tiresome, it's *so* easy to cast X aside and forget about it. It is much more effective to say to a friend, "I'm going to do X, please hold me to it." When you have a friend nagging you about X, it is harder to cast X aside. You naturally want to please your friend, or at least get him off your back, and that gives you more incentive to actually do X.

Final Encouragements

I hope you will find this advice helpful, especially if you are now going through a difficult time of unemployment. Remember that you are *more* than the job you hold, and you *can* make a difference in the world, even when you have no job. Remember also that this is a temporary phase in your life; it will end. I believe you can help yourself through this phase by not acting out of panic and by refusing to act due to fear.

Don't get down on yourself, and don't try to go it alone.

I want you to know that I am taking my own advice and learning from my mistakes. Even with the simple act of writing this essay, I am taking steps that, not long ago, I would have been too afraid to take.

I wish you the best of success in your job search or your business.

Thanks, Chuck. Readers will be happy to know Chuck is employed again, and he is writing the sequel to "On Dragon's Wings."

Now, bravely on to create your own action plan.

Chapter 9: **Create Your Action Plan**

You must *plan* to succeed. If you *fail* to plan, the saying goes, you *plan* to fail.

If you have accomplished the first three steps in this workbook, you now know three important things:
- You know you have what it takes.
- You know what service to provide (the best idea for you).
- You know where to work (your home office space).

As you create your action plan, you will commit to *when* you will accomplish each step along the way to being in business. First, let's get started by defining those steps. Think about the actions that will take you from today to the day when you will be making money from home while you continue your job search. Basic steps in your plan might include the following:

- Discuss your plans with your family.
- Get any training you might need.
- Obtain your business license.
- Research and purchase any insurance your business requires.
- Have business cards printed (see "Appendix B: Resources for Your Business").
- Research the competition and pricing for similar products or services in your area.
- Purchase first-time supplies in small quantities.
- Experiment with designs and create sample products or service packages.
- Try your product or service out on friends and relatives (or on actual potential customers).
- Finalize your product or service along with pricing, guarantees, and a customer service plan.
- Research and place your first ads and/or hand out flyers and/or implement your e-mail marketing strategy.
- Set up shop and start working!

Don't be discouraged by the list of action items. Once you reach that last step, you will be *in business*. You might be amazed at how one item builds on another. Soon you will have the momentum you need to carry you through.

Give yourself a serious pep talk once in a while or a swift kick in the pants if you can accomplish it, and keep moving. Now, customize your actual action plan below.

Your Action Plan

As you identify the steps needed to accomplish your plan, don't be concerned yet with which steps come first, second or last. Begin by using the two exercises below to list all of the necessary steps to start earning income. And please don't be intimidated by the number of things you have to do to get started. You'll be taking baby steps and getting encouragement here every step of the way.

Using both the *Target* exercise and the *Stair-steps* exercise will help you think of things you might miss if you only listed the steps once. Then it will be time for you to decide which steps come first, second, and so on, and to assign dates to them.

Worksheet: Target Exercise

Write your goal in the bull's eye; write, "I am in business," or the name of your business. Next, in the outermost circle, write the first few steps.

List some steps provided on the previous pages and some steps specific to the service you will provide.

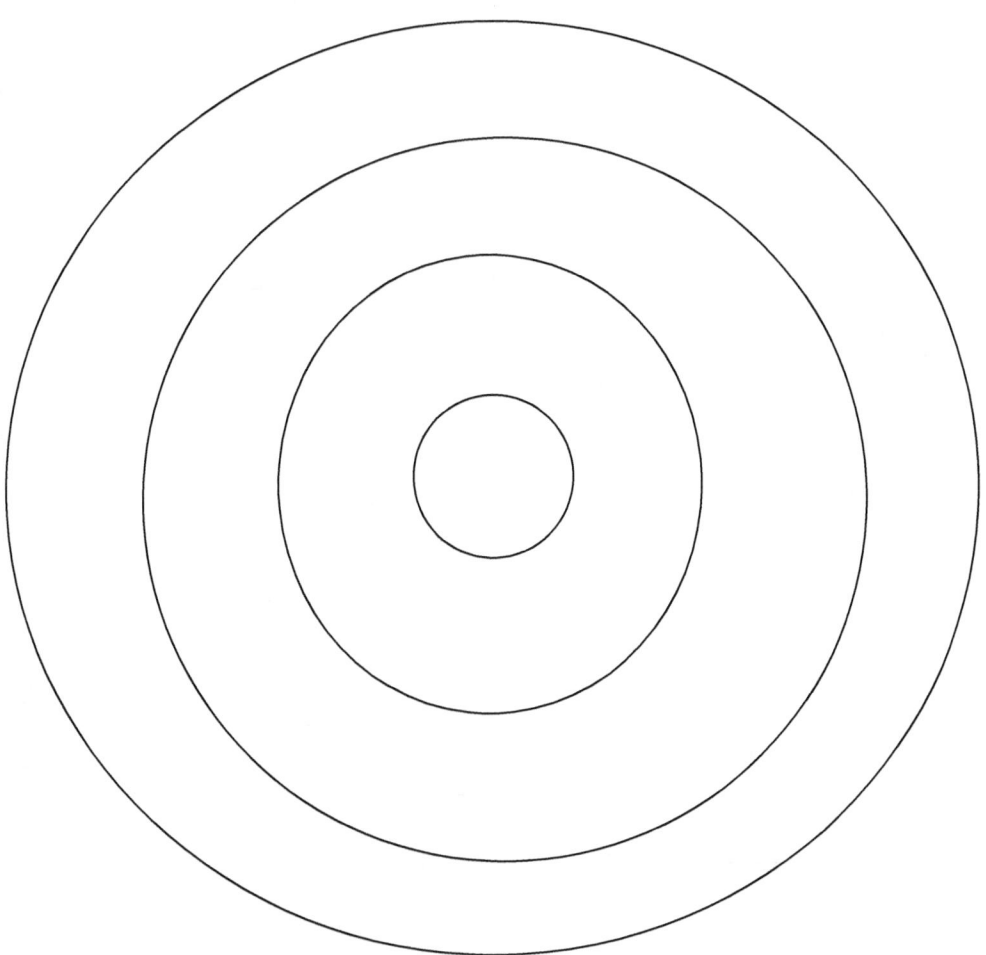

Worksheet: Stair-step Exercise

Start at the top of the stairs and write, "At the Bank". The goal of business is, after all, to make money, so the end-goal is regular trips to the bank to make deposits.

Now, write the items from your Target Exercise on the bottom stairs and fill in the stairs in an upward direction with action items specific to the service you will provide.

$$$

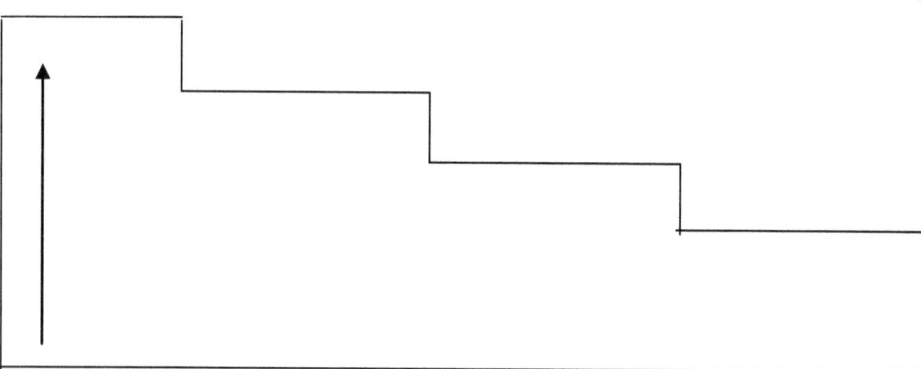

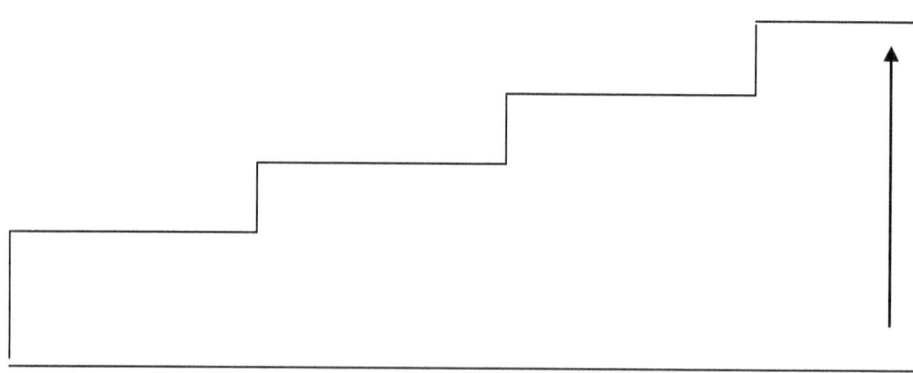

Your Task List

List the steps identified in the *Target* and *Stair-step* exercises in the table below. As you list them in the order in which they must be accomplished, new steps will occur to you. For instance, if you list, "place classified ad" you must also list, "*write* classified ad" as a sub-task, and tasks related to researching the best and most cost-effective publications for your ad, and free listings such as craigslist.org.

	Task	**Sub-task (if needed)**
1		
2		
3		
4		
5		
6		
7		
8		
9		
10		
11		
12		

Make copies of this page or use a planner if needed.

Next, get your calendar or use the one below and schedule a date for each task. Start with today and look at your first task. On what date will you start and by what date will you have that first task accomplished? Schedule the first several tasks on your calendar (these should be tasks that can be started and accomplished this week and within the following two weeks). Now, keep these appointments with yourself. You are making a date with your future. Keep that date!

Month:

Sunday	Monday	Tuesday	Wednesday	Thursday	Friday	Saturday

Month:

Sunday	Monday	Tuesday	Wednesday	Thursday	Friday	Saturday

As you accomplish the earlier tasks, you might have to adjust the dates for the later tasks on the worksheet. As you check-off each task you accomplish, you can add additional tasks from your worksheet to your calendar.

Play Now and Pay Later

This illustration will help you understand the consequences of your action and *inaction*. Imagine the specifics of your life as in the example below.

If I *Play* Now...	I Will *Pay* Later...
Sleep late	Roommate's snoring keeps me up
Take a long hot bath	Wait in line to use the bathroom
Visit with friends	Visit the woman in the next room at the State Old Folks' Home
Go shopping	Watch TV
Dinner at a restaurant	Beans for dinner again
Watch the late movie	Watch TV, Watch TV, Watch TV

However, if I am willing and disciplined enough to pay the price now, I can *play* later.

If I *Pay* Now...	I Can *Play* Later...
Up early and shower	Up early and to the hot tubs
Scan the paper for competitors' ads	Lounge by the pool, then shower
Makes sales calls	Visit a few shops
Go to a business class	Dinner with friends
Dinner with family or friends	Catch that new play
Stay up late rewriting sales letters	Meet at the cafe to end the evening

Learn to enjoy deferred gratification but reward yourself in small tangible but *affordable* ways when you reach important milestones.

Quit living by accident. *LIVE ON PURPOSE.*

In-box

```
    From: Big Bad Boss
      To: You
 Subject: Yell at yourself

Pretend you are your favorite coach from a
sports team or from your personal life and
give yourself a good talking to.

Yell at yourself about your current
situation. Give yourself a strong pep talk.
Tell yourself to get off the couch and to
GET TO WORK MAKING MONEY.

Use a few specifics so that the tirade is
meaningful.  Make your own Big Bad Boss
journal and write down your rants for future
inspiration.
```

The next step is to advertise, but with the help of an insider, I have first included a special section on publicity. Publicity is sometimes called "free advertising," but, as you will read, you must invest time and careful effort to publicize your business. The pay-off can be truly rewarding if you do it well.

Chapter 10: **The Truth About Publicity**

Wikipedia defines publicity as, "…the deliberate attempt to manage the public's perception of a subject," and it defines public relations (PR) as, "…a field concerned with maintaining public image for high-profile people, commercial businesses and organizations, non-profit associations or programs."

Wait a minute…what about us low-profile folks? You *can* get noticed by your local news organizations, and in rare cases, by national media, too.

There are several online services selling press-release writing and delivery services. Before you spend any money on them, read this.

Colin Flaherty, an award-winning journalist and publicist (see colinflaherty.com), has taught journalists for years, and has gone on assignment with them. He says that when reporters get together, the conversation frequently turns to "goofy PR people."

I have had limited success with releases, and Flaherty explains why my most recent one failed to garner results.

I recently used PRWeb.com to broadly distribute a release. When Flaherty asked me via e-mail, "May I ask what kind of reception your press release received?" my answer was, "Dismal."

Though Internet marketing courses recommend using press releases to improve search-engine results for your Web site, Colin's response was, "I would have said the results were going to be dismal ...not because of your release, BUT BECAUSE WE SHOULD NEVER USE PRESS RELEASES!"

When I phoned for more detail, he asked me, "When was the last time you read something that didn't have your name on it?" and "Why do people believe we can suspend rules of human communication with reporters?"

Flaherty, who says that the media is the most credible way to reach potential clients (rivaled only by enthusiastic customers), has been published in The New York Times, Time Magazine, and hundreds of other national and regional publications, and has appeared on local and national television shows, and garnered exposure for his clients there, too.

So what does he recommend, if not press releases? He says that purchasing a list of media contacts related to your business field, and addressing quick, targeted e-mails to reporters *by name* works. He uses a mail-merge program to make quick work of this process.

At the end of our phone conversation, he asked, "Do you watch the news?" I said I read my news online…Yahoo news, NYTimes.com, WashingtonPost.com, BostonHerald.com, and so on. He said, "Here is my final piece of advice: you are no longer a consumer of the news. You are now a manager of the news."

He explained that when I read a current news item related to my field, I should send a quick e-mail related to that story, tied to my business. I can let reporters know that there is a local angle to this news story.

I remembered that the last time I sent local releases, they were indeed addressed to specific people.

Flaherty recommends using Google Alerts (google.com/alerts) to receive e-mails related to my book. (News organizations also offer e-mailed alerts.) Then, when I receive a news story related to job loss, I can send a targeted e-mail to my local media contacts and to reporters who cover the topic nationally.

If you are not a writer, I highly recommend asking a friend to help you craft a few paragraphs describing the news angle of your business. Of course, when you can afford it, paying a professional for help to create your public image and news angle can, in some cases, be more effective than paying for advertising, but the best results come from a combined campaign that includes advertising, promotions, and media contacts.

Here's what worked for me in the past.

First, I wrote the release as if it were a short news blurb. (This was before I had Flaherty's advice.) Sometimes, the paper *will* print it as-is, so if you use this method, read some of the local news items and write your release in a similar style, keeping readers in mind. Ask yourself, "Why should they care?" to keep the focus on the benefit and impact on readers.

Next, I called every local newspaper and TV station and asked, "Can you tell me who should receive a release on X?" Then I asked for that person's e-mail address. I got a better response to e-mails than to faxes, though I know other professionals who get better responses to faxes. At the news stations, it will typically be the news desk that receives items. At the local papers, you should receive a specific editor's name.

Finally, I sent the release in the body of the e-mail text and as an attachment (in case they preferred one method over the other), although some places now block attachments due to the risk of receiving a virus that would harm their networks.

Whenever possible, refer them to your Web site, which can include as much detail as needed. (I use a simple drop-and-drag Web-site design tool with hosting that costs only a few dollars a month. That way, I don't have to contact a webmaster when I need to make updates to my site.)

My press releases have resulted in local TV and newspaper coverage for myself and for clients. Interestingly, when one release resulted in local television news coverage, being interviewed on camera was more fun than answering questions for the newspaper, but the newspaper story resulted in many, many more customers than the T.V. news story did.

I asked Flaherty for some final instruction and encouragement, and he quickly responded via e-mail. In his own words:

- "Reporters wake up in the morning wondering how they are going to find something new and unique and different and interesting to write about.
- "Marketing gurus ask almost the exact same questions: What is it about my product (or service) that is new, unique, different and beneficial?

"I'm not saying they are the same thing. They are not. But they are very closely related.

"So if you want to get into the newspaper/whatever, you have to bridge that gap.

"But here's the killer: *most business people kill their stories by sending out a press release,* instead of just sitting down and sending Johnnie or Mary a note saying, 'Hey, thought you might want to know that starting January 1, Charlotte real estate brokers are required to disclose if they are steering their deals to a certain mortgage banker' (or whatever).

"*That* is a story. *You* are the authority.

"That is a hell of a lot different than creating something called a press release, passing it around to everyone in your office, then ten days after the news is over, sending it out as a press release.

"I am not kidding; people do this.

"They sometimes hire people to do this, and when it doesn't work, they always have the same reason: reporters do not like business people.

"Here's the important part: The big benefit you will get from your press does not come from the day it is aired or printed. It will come when you incorporate it into your marketing materials.

"Press is really nothing but credible third-party testimonials.

"And you want to use it to increase your credibility with potential and existing customers so you can 1) Get a shot at more deals; 2) Close more deals faster.

"Maybe that means posting it on your Web site. Maybe that means incorporating it very quietly into an e-mail newsletter. Maybe that means giving out copies of your article before your sales meeting.

"Maybe that means getting your friends to spread it around to other reporters in the biz, hinting that this is a good story and hinting again that perhaps they should do something like that.

"Maybe that means sending it to blogs. Maybe that means posting it in your store.

"There is a lot of misunderstanding about message.

"For the press, a message is not 'We are the best restaurant in North Carolina.' That is an advertisement.

"A message is something about your business or industry that people can *use*.

When I get together with other PR people and we are comparing notches on our belts, I tell them that I got a barbeque restaurant on NPR (National Public Radio) for *one hour*.

"That ends our discussion.

"The message of everything in the press is this: 'Dang, that company/person is so important that the newspaper sought out his/her opinion for its story!'"

Thanks for that insight, Colin. Let's put it to good use. Remember that reporters are very busy people. Help them by providing quick information related to a story, and offer details that help them report real news.

Your Public Image

Today, of course, you must also manage the public perception of your business by managing your online presence. Because *you are* your company, your presence on social media sites such as Facebook, LinkedIn, Gather, Twitter and others may have an impact you weren't considering when you made comments you intended only for your "friends."

Be professional and courteous at all times, and consider creating accounts at those and other sites for your business name, too, when you have the time to build your presence online.

Next Steps

The next steps are to advertise and sell, which, of course, impact and involve your public image and relationships you build with the press, as we have just discussed.

Don't let fear stop you! My husband is one of my best encouragers, and as he says, the people who are out there making things happen are just like you and me.

Don't let perfectionism stop you. Do excellent work, but remember to ask yourself, as my husband asks himself, "Who are the people who will be judging you? They are people just like you and me."

I learned so much reading "The Courage to Write: How Writers Transcend Fear" by Ralph Keyes. I'll bet you didn't know that many of your favorite authors are chicken at times, just like you.

Keep your courage up, remember the rewards of action, and simply take the next steps.

Chapter 11: **Advertise**

A Forbes.com article about online advertising was titled, "Newspaper Killer" and you may know that the author, Louis Hau, was referring to Craigslist. It is sad and historically significant that we have lost and are losing landmark newspapers, but I remember the relatively high cost of classified advertising, and a listing on Craigslist is free.

Craigslist classified and other local online listings should be part of your advertising mix, but you will miss a significant number of potential customers if you exclude your local newspaper. (By the way, subscribe to your local paper today!)

Please, please be very cautious about investing money in advertising. Promise? If at all possible (and it usually is), earn some money in your chosen field and perfect your product or service before you place your first paid ad.

I remember a meeting of a few local freelance writers. Two of us had our Web sites created and business cards printed and our portfolios were full of work samples. The third writer said something like, "Oh, I know I should get business cards and a Web site. I've just been so busy with assignments." She did things in the right order. She called around and marketed her services before investing time or dollars in advertising. The other freelancer and I looked at each other and felt just a little bit stupid.

You are a Walking Ad

Since *you* are the company, you are also a walking, talking advertisement for your service. You want to be ready with a good answer when people ask, "And what do *you* do?" Of course, you might want to let people know you are in transition between jobs so you can enlist their help in finding a new position, but you also want to let them know about your new business effort.

Instead of stammering,

- "I take care of plants for companies," or,
- "I clean houses," or,
- "I sell cosmetics,"

…you can be prepared with a conversational answer that will whet their appetite for your product or service.

For the examples above, a descriptive paragraph might sound something like the following examples. (Inject your own personality to make it your very own.)

"I help people be more productive and creative at work by providing and maintaining indoor plants and trees. Since live plants are known to reduce stress and increase concentration, I advise big and small companies on the ideal indoor landscaping for their offices. Then I install the plants and keep them watered, fed and healthy. Sometimes I can even provide this service for just a single office, depending on the location."

"I sell peace, harmony, free time, pride, and good standing in the community. I clean houses and apartments so that my customers have more free time for themselves *and* take more pride in their homes. A well ordered home also promotes better discipline with children and more romance between husband and wife! When folks are thinking about using my services, I help them identify the cleaning plan that suits them best and fits into their budgets. This week, I'm doing a half-price special."

"I work with women to help them look their best. I represent (name of cosmetic company) and I consult with my clients to help them find the best combination of products for the image they want to project. I offer a free stress-reducing facial and make-over, too."

Try to end your paragraph with a question to get the listener involved. For instance, "Do you have live plants where you work?" or "Have you ever tried a home-cleaning service? or "What do you find most challenging when shopping for cosmetics?"

The goal is not to memorize and repeat your descriptive paragraph like a parrot. That will only result in funny looks and quick excuses. Your goal is to entice people to want to know more. In many cases, almost everyone you talk to will be a potential client or will know someone who is. Once you have crafted your descriptive paragraph, you will be able to talk naturally about the product or service you provide in a way that makes people want to know more.

Craft your Descriptive Paragraph

Use this space to write, rewrite, and think out your own descriptive paragraph. If a blank page makes you nervous, start on scrap paper and write down your final draft here.

Descriptive Paragraph

Before you spend your first advertising dollar, you should know as much as possible about the market you are trying to reach, and about the companies in your area that are already servicing that market. If you are starting a home daycare center, your market research can be as simple as looking through the classified ads for childcare in your local paper. Call to find a local daycare provider willing to share information on the going rate for part-time and fulltime care, what kind of response to expect from an ad, what kind of turnover they experience, and so on. Since each daycare provider needs only a few children to support his or her business, competition is not a concern, and most providers won't mind discussing the details of the business with you.

If your business will be in direct competition with similar local businesses, the owners might not be willing to share such details with you. In that case, try to find someone in a nearby town with whom you won't be in direct competition, who is willing to give you the ins and outs of the business, and perhaps some secrets to success.

Another simple source of market information is your potential customers. For the daycare business, ask mothers you know how they meet their childcare needs. People are usually glad to answer your questions, and you might be able to turn a few of these inquiries into your first clients.

If your business is in a field that typically advertises in the Yellow Pages™ or the online equivalent, look there for details about existing companies in your field. In some cases this can be misleading, however. When I started writing freelance business material from home, I found very few ads for these services in the phone directory. This might have led me to believe that there weren't many of these service providers available in the area, but I found that most businesses of that type advertised in the local paper with classified ads.

One of my favorite sources of inside information is the trade magazines published for most industries. Trade magazines are not intended to be read by the general public. They are published for business owners and professionals within a certain industry. Your local research librarian can help you find one or more trade magazines for your chosen business field.

One final source of information is the association for your type of business. Your library should have a copy of the "Encyclopedia of Associations" with listings by category of industries. Ongoing market research will keep you informed of the latest trends in the industry you have chosen. As you research, jot down any ideas that occur to you concerning new and different ways to reach your target customers, as well as ideas for new or improved products or services to meet their needs.

What Should You Say in your Ad?

You can advertise with more success than many business owners if you will remember that your potential customers are always asking, "What's in it for me?" So when they see an ad that says, "Joe's Auto Detailing," they just turn the page unless they are *already* in the market for detailing services. You want to make people who were looking for grocery coupons suddenly desire auto-detailing services, from *you*.

If, on the way to the grocery coupons, they see an ad that says, "Turn their heads," or, "Look at That Car!" readers instantly know what's in it for them...a car that will be the envy of their friends. They are much more likely to read on to discover what will make their car so attractive.

Once you have your readers' attention you must give them a "call to action". Tell them to call today for a free estimate, and to receive their free winter car-care tips. If you are providing home day care, state the facts as your competitors' ads do, but spend a few extra dollars to include a benefit in your ad. "Learning activities prepare your child for school" or "A cuddly home atmosphere." These promises will increase the response you receive if the other ads simply state the hours and cost of care.

Call your local newspapers and ask them to send you a display advertising rate sheet (for the larger ads in the main body of the newspaper) or a classified ad rate sheet. Create a folder for each publication. Be sure to ask callers where they saw your advertisement if you place an ad in more than one publication, so you will know which paper is more effective.

Important Note
Several smaller ads placed in successive days' papers are far more effective than a one-time larger ad. Readers typically need to see an ad several times before they respond to it.

After-the-Sale Advertising

After-the-sale advertising is so effective and inexpensive that I don't know why more companies don't use it. Have you ever bought an item and then opened it at home to find a small note enclosed that says something like this: "You have purchased a quality product that will be a treasured part of your family for years. Our skilled artisans have invested their best efforts to create the exact detail and exceptional value that you now hold in your hands. Use our product in good health, and may it bring you years of pleasure."

I don't know about you, but something like this makes me want to go out and buy three more to give as gifts. This kind of advertising is more believable because it is not trying to convince you to buy something; it *confirms* your choice. It makes you feel smart for buying that item.

When you use this method, be sure to include an order form along with the note, to encourage repeat sales. Here are a few ways you can incorporate this very effective form of advertising.

Cleaning Business - Leave a note on pretty paper on your client's kitchen table, or on the receptionist's desk. Once in a while, leave a flower, too. Say something like, "I enjoyed working in your home / office today. Please let me know if there is something special you need me to take care of next time."

Cosmetics Company - Send a note in the mail. Make it your own, but your brief note might say, "Thank you for choosing an X-company product. My personal service means you get my best efforts and news about the latest trends. Best of all ... no more wasted make-up. If you are not satisfied, just let me know and I will ..."

Home Daycare - Every day, write a note on a bright index card saying something like, "I so much enjoyed working with child-name today. S/he played with child-name, and we all sang the song-name song."

You could add a positive quotation, too. Keep it light, positive, and professional. This level of personal service is the next evolution in customer expectations, and it can mean more business for you. More importantly, it can mean happier clients, which makes you a happier service provider.

Advertising Specialties

You probably have several advertising specialties in your kitchen or on your desk. The calendar from a Realtor, the magnet from your insurance broker...these are advertising specialties, and you can use them, too. Based on the number of times you have called a phone number printed on one of these products, you might think that these items were a waste of the advertisers' money. But a pen that costs twenty cents could generate a fifty-dollar order. At that rate, you could receive only one order from 250 pens and still break even.

If that customer becomes a repeat customer or refers another customer to you, you are way ahead of the game. Look in a local business listing under "Advertising" or talk to your local printer about pricing and products available.

Free Advertising

Here are a few ways to advertise when you have little or no money to invest. Of course, advertising on Craigslist.com should be part of your campaign.

Cross-Advertising

Look for opportunities to exchange advertising exposure with a related company that is not in competition with your product or service. For instance, an interior decorator might give your maid-service flier to her clients, and you in turn could give her brochure to your clients. You both get free exposure to a targeted customer base.

Word-of-Mouth

Positive word-of-mouth advertising is by far the best form of free advertising. Think about how you find a mechanic, a computer technician, or a new doctor or dentist. You ask your friends, neighbors, and coworkers for a name they trust, don't you? When you provide your product or service in such an excellent manner that people remember you, you will generate positive word-of-mouth advertising without even asking for it.

You should ask for it, however. Remember to ask your hugely satisfied customers to spread the word to *their* friends, family, coworkers and neighbors.

The negative side of this form of free advertising is that it can kill you. Think back to the last time you were upset by the treatment you received at a local business. If they ruined your favorite dress and said that *you* did it, or they said they were open until five, but they closed just as you arrived at 4:50, how many people did you tell about your bad experience? The unfortunate truth is that, when we (and our customers) are dissatisfied, we typically tell ten or more people about the horrible experience we had. But when we are satisfied, we tell no one, or perhaps just one person, about what a good job was done.

So be sure to do more than the customer expects, and then don't forget to ask them to help spread the word.

Hold a Drawing

Have you ever seen one of those boxes on the counter when you are ordering your sandwich or paying for your drugstore purchase? There is usually a pile of tiny forms where you can add your name, address, and phone number to drop into the box. One person wins two free weeks at the local gym, and everyone else gets a call to see if they'd like to have a one-day free trial (with sales pitch). Could you make this work for your product or service? You could offer a free facial if you are selling cosmetics, or a free plant if you are an indoor landscaper. Only people who would enjoy the free product register, so you could end up with many qualified leads, and of course your winner could turn into a client.

Free Samples

Offering potential customers free samples is a very effective advertising tool. However, they are never "free" to you. They will cost you time, effort, and whatever your wholesale cost of the product is. But again, if you give ten free samples and get one new customer, you should come out ahead, especially when you provide such excellent service that the new customer becomes a customer for life.

E-mail List

It used to be that, no matter who you were, if you wanted to get the word out to potential customers you had to have a budget for paper, envelopes, and postage. E-mail is probably the most cost-effective method of reaching people. However, sending e-mails to folks whom you do not know (called spamming) is *not* good business. Instead, offer an opt-in e-mail list.

If you have information to offer, such as super-fast house-cleaning tips, or plant-care-made-easy, or simply my-weekly-specials, do a bit of research (see "Appendix B: Resources for Your Business") and start an e-mail group or e-newsletter. Of course, in addition to providing short, interesting information tidbits, you will promote your product or service and make it very, very easy for readers to contact you and to order your service.

Web Site

Danger! Danger! Carefully limit the time you allow yourself to create your Web site. You may not need a site when you are just starting out, though it has become almost as expected as (and in some cases *more* expected than) business cards. Unless it will be your primary marketing tool, you can create a one or two-page site, sometimes called a brochure site. A blog can also act as your business site, in some cases.

Yola.com and Blogger.com are two free resources. If you plan to create a site yourself, take the time you need to thoroughly learn the interface, and promise yourself that you won't get discouraged. You can do it! It takes time but this investment in time and effort will help you gain up-to-date, marketable skills.

This is where you can include more details so that when you send a note to the local media, reporters and editors can go online to learn more about your business. Potential customers who see your classified ad or flyer can also go to your site to learn more about you and your service, and to decide if you look trustworthy and worthy of their patronage.

I recently created a simple site for a friend's business and after about a month he said, "It hasn't brought us any business." *Now* I have learned that I should have told him to submit a local listing to Yahoo! Search and Google Maps, but I also should have told him that typically, a Web site is like a business card. You have to *give* it to people. Another friend uses her site to help sell her property. When people answer her classified ad, she is able to refer them to the site for specifications, pictures and directions.

Search-engine optimization (adding content and links to your site to help it rank higher in search results online, and several other actions you can and should take) is effective, but it takes a lot of time. When you can budget the time and/or marketing dollars, visit TenGoldenRules.com for excellent, current information. Jay Berkowitz, founder of Ten Golden Rules, is one of the instructors in the online marketing course I am taking, and I recommend his company and the information he offers (much of which *is* free).

I keep hearing the phrase, "Content is king!" related to Web sites and online marketing. To create a professional presence, *and* to help you rank higher in search-engine results, you *must* have very well written content in what I call Web-bite-size paragraphs. Unless you are a professional writer, you should find help to create your content.

Look for little ways to spread the word about your product or service and if you are consistent and persistent, you should see results start to roll in.

In-box

```
  From: Big Bad Boss
    To: You
Subject: !!!

KEEP WORKING.

Don't slow down now.  Speed it up a notch.
You know you can do this!  You are the only
one who can say what you need to say.

NO ONE ELSE CAN SAY IT LIKE YOU DO.
NO ONE ELSE CAN MAKE IT LIKE YOU DO.
NO ONE ELSE CAN SELL IT LIKE YOU DO.

Remember past successes.  Use humor.  Find
something funny to watch or read every day,
or hang out with a funny friend.

GENERATE SOME NEW ENERGY AND POUR IT INTO
YOUR PROJECT TODAY.

What you have accomplished stays
accomplished.  Now build on that!!!
```

Worksheet: Advertising Plan

Some of the methods in this table are described on later pages. Once you have established your marketing plan, stick with it. Jay Conrad Levinson, in one of his original *Guerrilla Marketing* books, said that sticking with it is one of the keys to the success of your plan.

TYPE OF ADVERTISING	My Specific Plan
Word-of-Mouth	
Calling for Clients	
Flyers	
Notes to media	
Cross-advertising	
Classified ads	
Display ads	
Web site	
After-the-Sale Advertising	

Jot down advertising ideas that occur to you, remembering to answer your potential customers' all-important question, "What's in it for me?" And remember to use the best kind of advertising there is: referrals. Ask every customer whom he or she knows who might also enjoy your product or service.

Chapter 12: **Sell (Yes, you *can!*)**

"Sell? I'm no salesperson! If I have to sell something, forget it!" If this is how you feel, you are not alone. Selling has a bad reputation, yet you have been doing it all of your life. Every time you convinced your Mom to let you have one more cookie, or watch one more TV show before bed, you were "selling" her on your wishes. Selling gets a bad name when a pushy salesperson is rude. But think about all the times in your life when a salesperson was helpful. Good salespeople outnumber the bad ones by a long shot, and you can be one of them.

Think of selling as simply following up. When people ask you what you do, you are simply following up by answering their questions about your product or service. When someone answers your classified ad, you are following up on his interest in what you have to offer. When someone stops by your booth at the craft fair, you are following up on her interest by describing what you have to sell, and by asking questions about her needs.

Plan your follow-up process to take advantage of the very first time someone shows interest in your product or service. Role-play with a friend or family member and go through the sequence of events as if a customer is responding to your ad. Practice all the way through to the end, until the sale or service is completed. Doing this will help you identify the sequence of actions you will need to take once you get that first response.

You can take it a few steps further and role-play a follow-up call to your customer to be certain he or she is satisfied, and even try to create some repeat business or try to get a referral for a new customer. If you don't have someone to role-play with, rehearsing this scenario in your imagination can be almost as effective in helping you anticipate the different avenues of response you might get from potential customers. Do this enough times and your first potential customer will think you've been in business for years.

Features and Benefits

The example of a classified ad for a home daycare center in the previous chapter included the sentence, "Learning activities prepare your child for school." Helping a child prepare for school is a *benefit* of the "learning activities" *feature*. Would the phrase, "comfy home atmosphere" be a feature or a benefit? If you said "feature", you are right. The *benefit* of a comfy home atmosphere might be that children will feel relaxed and happy.

Whether you use telemarketing, sales letters, or classified ads, it is most effective to include the features *and* benefits of your product or service. Review the following list of features and benefits to become more familiar with the difference between the two. This can be a challenge even for seasoned sales professionals, and once you have it mastered, you could be well on your way to selling success.

Feature	Benefit
We care for your plants weekly.	You never have to water a dying plant again.
We do weekly grocery shopping for you.	You have more time for yourself.
Our toys are educational.	Your children learn while they play.
Wrong shade? Return it for a refund.	No more wasted money and unused bottles of cosmetics in your cabinet.

As you can see, the benefit answers that all-important question, "What's in it for me?" Complete the *Features & Benefits* worksheet and then keep those benefits in mind as you learn about the different methods of finding new customers on the following pages.

Worksheet: Features & Benefits

First list several features of your product or service, then write down the benefit associated with each feature.

This exercise will help you understand why someone would want to purchase your product or service.

Feature	Benefit

Calling Future Clients

If you will be calling potential customers on the telephone, here are some tips that, if followed, will help the people on the other end of the phone enjoy the conversation. If you don't think calling potential clients is effective, read *The Well-fed Writer* by Peter Bowerman or go to WellFedWriter.com to learn how one writer turned a plan into profit with his phone, his creativity, and professional follow-up.

If the term "telemarketing" has occurred to you, let me point out the ways in which you differ from a telemarketer. You are a local service provider letting local individuals or businesses know about the products or services you can provide. Think about how *you* might feel if one of your neighbors called to let you know he or she was opening a registered daycare around the corner or providing home and office cleaning services. You might be very happy to get the call if it is a service you need, and if not, you might be able to pass the caller's information on to a friend in need of those services.

Relax and enjoy getting in touch with local people as you contact potential future clients. Follow these simple tips to help you and your potential clients get the most out of each call.

1. Get permission to proceed.

When someone answers the phone you will identify yourself and then ask for permission to proceed. This doesn't mean you have to ask if this is a good time to call or whether the person has time to talk to you, although you might want to use those methods. Permission to proceed might be as simple as the person on the other end of the line saying, "Uh huh."

Example: "This is Donna Buskirk, a local instructor. Have I reached Women Working After 50?" Once the person who answered says, "Yes," I have received permission to keep talking. What you want to avoid here is the mistake some telemarketers make...going into a non-stop sales pitch like the following.

Never say this: "Hello, I'm Sam Smooth with the Better Life Foundation and we are running a special today on our best-selling products including items that can enhance your life right away. We offer several packages for every income bracket, plus easy payment plans. The first offer is..." Can't you just hear the *click* as you hang up on Sam? He did *not* have your permission to keep talking.

Instead, say something like this (Sam could easily have gotten permission by simply pausing after identifying himself): "Hello, I'm Sam Smooth with the Better Life Foundation (pause)". If the caller says, "Yeah?" Sam has received permission to keep talking. Then, if he wants to avoid being hung up on, he needs to phrase his sales pitch in questions, not in a run-on monologue.

2. Reach the decision-maker.

If I am talking to a very friendly person who is willing to listen and likes everything about my product or service, I have completely wasted my time unless that person is the decision-maker. The receptionist might love what I have to offer, but if she can't buy the product, who cares?

Example: Me - "This is Donna Buskirk, a local instructor. Have I reached Women Working After 50?"

Receptionist - "Yes."

Me - "Can you tell me who books the speakers for your organization's meetings?"

You then ask to speak with that person. If he or she is not in, ask for the best time to reach that person, and leave a message that you will be calling back at that time. Then don't fail to call. Consider it an appointment and be prepared to sell.

Frequently, screening calls is part of the receptionist's job. His or her mission might be to keep you from bothering the boss. This person can also become your biggest ally. Be sincerely nice. But if he or she tells you, "That would be my boss, but he's on the phone," then your response should be, "Oh, OK, I'll hold. *Thank* you." with a big smile in your voice. Saying *thank you* sends a signal that helps the person do what you have already thanked them for. (If you have young children, try this on them. Sometimes it works like magic to make *thank you* part of the command. "Johnny, give that to your sister now. Thank you." Then watch him obey.)

3. Make the offer.

Use your descriptive paragraph to help describe what it is you have to offer. Ask questions to discover the needs of your prospect, and remember to describe the benefits of your product or service. Decide ahead of time if you are going to ask for the sale, or for an appointment, or simply to prepare your prospect to receive a sales letter from you.

Example: "Mrs. Hale, I conduct workshops on a variety of subjects that I think your members would enjoy. Tell me, does your organization hire speakers from time to time? ... It's a fast-paced fun workshop. Attendees use games, worksheets and exercises to find the best moneymaking enterprise for them. Does this sound like something that would interest your members? ... I conduct a two-hour workshop, or a thirty-minute mini-seminar. Which would best suit your needs? ... What available dates do you have in the next three months?"

Have fun doing a few role-play simulations with a friend or relative. If this makes you nervous, try putting on a fake accent, or try intentionally doing a really bad job. Having some fun with the practice in that way will help you get over the jitters. Then you might be surprised to find that you were more nervous practicing with your friend than you are when calling actual potential customers.

Use the *Calling Future Clients* worksheet to draft an outline of your approach.

Worksheet: Calling Future Clients

Remember to ask questions to discover the needs of the busy people you call. Be yourself, be professional and courteous, and have fun as you find those folks who need your product or service.

1. Get permission to proceed. **Starter**: This is X from/with X. I'm calling local X… (pause until s/he says, "Yes?").
2. Reach the Decision Maker. **Starter**: Can you tell me who handles the decisions on X?
a. Use your Descriptive Paragraph. **Starter**: Hello, I understand you X (pause for permission to proceed from this new person). I provide X.
b. Ask questions to discover his or her needs. **Starter**: What do you find is your biggest challenge when looking for X?
c. Mention the specific features & benefits that meet that need. **Starter**: I see. So you're saying X. I have/provide X that will X.
3. Make the Offer. **Starter**: I'd like to ask for fifteen minutes of your time to show you how X will meet your need for X. Would Wednesday or Thursday work for you?

Use this sheet to help you when you call potential clients, but *please don't* read from this material when you call. You will sound phony. Memorize your phrases and then simply say them in a natural conversational tone.

Writing for Customers

The primary advantage you have over big business is your ability to customize for each of your potential clients. Whether you use post cards, sales letters, e-mail, or a combination of these, you can cut through the litter of advertising by personally addressing your potential customers' concerns.

It used to be that mailing brochures and sales letters were the only way to reach potential clients, and it was a fairly expensive endeavor. Today, it doesn't cost you any additional money to send an e-mail to a potential customer, once you have the basic service set up. Creating a Web site is very affordable, too. However, because all of these methods are very affordable, everyone is using them and often there is little thought given to the content of these items. Many Web designers do an excellent job of making a site look professional without working with professional writers to ensure equally excellent content.

A sales letter can make or break your professional reputation. So can a post card or an e-mail. There are several excellent books on writing sales letters, and I recommend you study one, or have a professional write or edit your content. Incorrect grammar and misspelled worlds can spell disaster.

Would you like to take a shortcut? Find a book or Web site that provides templates, and customize from there. Then be sure to have someone who loves the English language proof your content before you send it out. Once you have a template with a few paragraphs and some basic organization, you can customize to your heart's content.

Here are a few tips to get you started. If you do hire a professional, it might save you some money to create a rough draft to provide the writer with the basics, so these tips are useful whether you plan to write your own sales letter or e-mail, or hire a professional.

Personalize your letter. Big companies can't afford to do this. They send out form-sales letters to thousands of prospective customers. You have the advantage. You can get to know each prospect and send an individualized letter that is much more likely to get a response.

Start in the middle. Ever heard of writer's block? It is very common to develop writer's block when you are staring at a blank piece of paper or a blank screen and you know that potential clients will eventually be reading your words. The beginning of the letter is crucial, but please forget about it. Start in the middle, with a scribbled list of benefits you offer. Once you get going, keep going. Later, you can decide which benefit or what question should start your letter to keep your prospects reading.

Ask for action. Don't simply describe how wonderful your product or service is and leave your reader nodding her head. Give her something to do and a reason to do it. Urge her to "call today for your free estimate of creative landscape designs for *your* yard." Here are a few examples.

"Call to receive your free tips on how to grow your grass and garden in the hard earth in this area."

"Call me to set up an appointment at your convenience. If you call this week, I'll give you 50% off my first week's service!"

"Contact me to ask about the free business-card design I offer when I create your first brochure or sales letter."

P.S.

Sales professionals have found that the P.S. at the end of a sales letter is what many people tend to read first, so that might be the ideal spot for your call to action. Sending a follow-up post card or e-mail a week after you send your original letter can also increase your responses.

Exercise: Stop throwing out the junk mail you receive and study it instead. Pay attention to what works and what doesn't. What is it about this particular envelope or letter that make you want to open it, or would you typically have tossed it?

Now, start to draft your own sales letter campaign, remembering to personalize each letter for maximum results.

As a final help, read these examples of what I mean by personalizing your content.

Instead of, "We provide landscaping service," say, "We love the landscaping at the entrance of the Deerfield community. We have customized landscaping plans that would complement your home while making your lawn and garden a true reflection of your taste. Call us for..."

Instead of, "Licensed Childcare Facility," say, "Loving home daycare for children in the Middle Creek Elementary area, serving families who live and work in Cary, Apex, and Holly Springs."

Instead of, "Business Writing Services," say, "I have come up with a few ideas for your Web site that I think will draw in potential clients and a specific value-add for your existing clients. I would enjoy the opportunity to discuss these with you in a brief 15-minute presentation..."

Worksheet: Writing for Customers

Tip: Start in the middle. Thinking that someone might actually read what you write might cause writer's block. Just start scribbling or make a list of points to cover. The opening line might be the last thing you write.

Write as if you are writing to a friend and invite your reader to learn more about how your product or service can meet a need.

Dear Neighbor:

Closing the Sale

There are dozens of excellent books devoted to "closing the sale." Once you have made your offer, you must ask your prospective customer to buy. Closing is the part of the selling process that makes the difference between success and no success. Use the following tips to get started, and when you are ready to move ahead, read a few good books on the subject and refine your technique.

1. Ask for the sale. Don't ask *if* they want it. Ask *when* they want it. What you have to offer is so good, you know they are going to want it, so ask what size, what color, how many. Be sensitive to your potential clients' needs so that you don't become pushy. When you can sense that your audience likes what you have to offer and just hasn't made that commitment yet, phrases like those below can help them start nodding and saying, "Yes" to your offer.

"If I can have it delivered tomorrow, would that be quick enough for you?" "When would you like me to get started?" "Would you like me to do the upstairs, too, or just the downstairs?" "Which of these plants do you think would be in your reception area?" "There is a training meeting tomorrow, and one on Saturday. Which would be best for you?" "If the color you choose is wrong, I'll bring by a free replacement. How does that sound?"

2. Think of objections as questions. Either during your presentation or when you are closing the sale, most prospective customers will have an objection. "But I can't afford that right now." Think of each objection as a question. Translate the above to, "How can I afford it?" Then answer the objection/question with a solution.

I can't afford it / How can I afford it? "You can make weekly payments." Or, "When you think about it, it works out to one dollar a day, and it could increase your business. Just one new customer would pay for the service."

I don't know if I could do something like that / How could I do something like that? "You will never know until you try. Everything new is a little scary at first. Why don't I arrange for you to talk to someone like you who was also scared to get started?"

I already buy mine at a discount store / Why should I buy yours instead? "I can offer you personal service, save you time shopping, and guarantee your purchase every time. Most stores don't accept returns of slightly used makeup, but I do. You can return or replace anything that isn't just right for you. And I know you'll enjoy our sales, discounts and free gifts with purchase.

Use the *Ask for the Sale* worksheet to practice your technique.

Worksheet: Ask for the Sale

Remember a time when you were excited about a purchase. You *wanted* to buy the service or item, and you were happy to complete the deal. Imagine that your potential customer is happy to hear your question, and ask for the sale!

Draft your deal-clinching phrases here. You won't be reading them to your potential clients; you will be using these phrases in conversation. But writing them down and reviewing them will help you work them into your conversation naturally.

Closing Questions and Statements:

Share the Excitement; Don't Show Fear

Your enthusiasm is the most important ingredient in any sales transaction. This is one reason why you must provide a product or service about which you are passionate. But even when you love the product or service, *fear* can slither in and smother that spark of excitement.

Try to imagine the reaction to your sales pitch if you let your fear show instead of displaying your excitement.

If you ask potential customers, "Would you like to try this?" while you are thinking, "*What* am I doing? You don't want to try this, do you?" they can sense the emotion behind your words and they answer, "No thanks." But when your emotions are saying, "This is *great*. You've just *got* to try it," the answering emotion in your customers is, "*What's* great? Why is it great?" They can't help but join your excitement and they want to learn more.

No matter how great the product or service, you will probably still hear more no-thank-you's than yes's, and this is the time to give yourself a pep talk. Just before each phone call or on the drive to meet with the prospect, tell yourself what a wonderful product or service you are offering, and remind yourself that you are getting better and better at making the presentation each and every time. You are about to offer the prospect a solution that will be an exciting problem solver, and the prospect will probably be really excited to hear what you have to say.

Remind yourself that you are unique in this world, and no one else can do exactly what you do. Even if you don't make a sale, you have made a new acquaintance and probably made that person smile. You know you might get more no's than yes's, but the yes's add up to success and you are going to succeed. If this prospect says no, maybe he or she knows someone who can use your services.

Give yourself a pep take before every sales call to build your enthusiasm and watch your business grow.

In-box

From: Big Bad Boss
To: You
Subject: You've got it

Time marches on, so don't slow down for a minute. Rest when you need to and stay in close touch with family and friends but GET THAT WORK DONE.

Take advantage of little pockets of time. Invest in your project with every available snatch of motivation and watch it grow toward completion.

As a creative type, you will have ebb and flow that sometimes makes you think you are slacking. DON'T be a slacker, but don't confuse the seasons of an artist's mood with slacking, either.

What you do stays done. What is written stays written. Build on what you have done before, without looking back.

GET TO WORK. You've got what it takes.

Chapter 13: **Build Your Business**

The job market being what it is today, you might want to continue providing a local service on the side when you start your next job. Even as a part-time effort, you can increase your profits step by step. Remember, it is your actions that can make this happen. You can make these steps as simple or as detailed as you like. For now, let's keep it simple. Start with the first small step and work from there.

Quality

One of the best ways to build your business once you get started is to sell to your current and past customers. Of course, this will only work when they are truly happy with the product or service they purchased. Although yours will be a very small business run from your home, your product or service must often compete with products and services produced by much larger companies. Quality must always be high. After all of your hard work, it would be a shame to lose repeat business because your quality is less than excellent. You should always be looking for ways to improve the quality and value of your product or service.

I like this advice I read several years ago: Make it your very best, and when you are done, go back and find ways to make it ten percent better. Apply this advice to your product or service, and you can't go wrong.

One very basic concept is to give your customers more than they expect. This can be a very simple thing, like the extra donut with a dozen, or a personal thank-you note with an order, or it can be something that costs you a little more, like a free item with a purchase, or a coupon to receive every fifth purchase at half price, assuming your profit margin allows that.

Use the Quality Worksheet to list several ways in which you can increase the quality of your product or service. Think of yourself as the customer, and list the level of quality *you* would expect. Don't be realistic at this stage...get creative and list even unrealistic expectations, such as a new car with each car-air-freshener you purchase. You can narrow them down later, but this all-out thinking process might help you identify a practical service that will really set your business apart.

Example: If you are selling cosmetics, you might wish for a personal makeover every morning before work. If you are teaching sewing workshops, you might wish that the instructor would sew a custom wardrobe for you. These unrealistic expectations might spark an idea that your customers would love. What about a free glamour makeover before a Saturday-night date for your customers? Or how about adding wardrobe consultation to your sewing services? In each case, the result could be happier customers, more free word-of-mouth advertising as they talk about the great deal they received, and more profits for you.

Before getting started on the worksheet below, think about two customer-service nightmares from your own shopping or service experience and write down two actions from each experience that would have made you a happier customer. What actions could the service provider have taken, or what could he or she have said, that would have resulted in a better outcome for you *and* for them?

Remember the saying, "The customer is always right?" Well, we know that's not true. My perspective is, "The customer is *not* always right, so it is our job to make the customer feel great about the transaction, even when he or she is wrong." You might say, "...*especially* when he or she is wrong," because you don't want them to bad-mouth your product or service all over town. How many people did you tell about *your* customer-service nightmare? Think about it.

Worksheet: Quality

Quality is a very simple concept that doesn't need a lot of explaining, but it does require a lot of serious attention on your part. Quality can make or break your business.

Have fun listing ways to improve the quality of your product or service on the following worksheet.

If I were the customer, I would want:

Realistic ways to improve my quality:

Customer Service

Think about the last time you enjoyed a really good meal at a restaurant. How many friends did you tell about your meal? Now, think about the last time you were spitting mad about the rotten service you received at a store, on a train, in a restaurant, or from a service provider. How many friends did you tell about *that* episode?

Surveys show that dissatisfied customers will tell ten or more people about their bad experiences. When you are really mad, you might even tell strangers who will listen never to go to that place. It is worth your extra effort to turn any dissatisfied customer into a very, very happy customer. How do you do that? Simply by putting yourself in his or her shoes (this means totally forgetting that this is your business, that you are right and the customer is wrong, and that the customer is a jerk anyway) and then doing *more* for that customer than you would expect if you were that customer.

I remember reading another interesting fact. In my four years of customer satisfaction research during the time when I was teaching customer service courses, one survey asked customers to rate their satisfaction levels with a catalog company. Who do you think gave a higher satisfaction rating?

- The customer for whom everything went smoothly.
- The customer who experienced a problem with an order that was later resolved.

Surprisingly, customers who experienced problems *and resolutions* were more satisfied than those who never experienced problems with their orders. If you think about it, when you are dealing with a new company, you are happy as long as nothing goes wrong, but how do you know what will happen if something *does* go wrong? Those survey results indicate that once you have personal experience with the company's excellent problem-resolution policy, you will feel even more comfortable dealing with them than before there was a problem, because you have proof that they handle problems to your satisfaction.

Bottom line? Turn dissatisfied customers into your best customers ever.

PS: Is the customer always right? No, of course not. But your business will be much, much more successful if you help even those customers who are wrong to feel really good about every experience they have with you. Give them more than they expect, and they could be your best source of advertising.

Establish Your Customer-Service Policy

Think ahead about how you will handle your customers' concerns. Ask yourself, "What if?"

- What if a customer uses half of your product and wants to return the rest?
- What if a customer wants special delivery?
- What if the product is broken by your customer's two-year-old, and she wants to know if you will replace it free of charge?
- What if you run out of an item that has been offered for sale, and potential customers are angry?
- What if plants are missing from the office and they want them replaced?
- What if they think you didn't clean the windows thoroughly?

Sometimes it is worth losing money and time on one deal to make one happy customer. That customer is then likely to do business with you again, and the ten people he or she *didn't* tell about how incompetent your service was are free to form their own opinions. It might be more profitable, in the end, to give the customer who used half of your product a full refund and a coupon good for half off the cost of a future purchase. For the angry people who traveled to your booth at the fair only to discover you are out of the advertised item, apologize and take names and numbers, promising to call when the item is again available, and offering it at an even bigger discount, or with a give-away thrown in. Then be sure to follow through, and keep them posted on any delays.

Complaints are Good

A customer's complaints are worth a lot to you, since most customers keep their gripes to themselves and their friends. Picture yourself in the store standing in line, frustrated that you found only half of the items you needed and wishing there was somewhere to sit while you waited to pay. Do you tell the cashier or ask for the manager? Probably not. You want to be nice, and you're in a hurry. But how is the storeowner going to know what products to add if you don't complain?

You might ask your own customers something like this: "If there was one way in which I could improve my service (or my product), what would that be?" And for those who complain without being asked, thank them for taking the time to complain. Chances are there are ten other customers out there with the same complaint who never said a word, and *now* you can address the issue.

Low Expectations

We have apparently grown to expect only fair quality from the products and services we buy and use every day. One of my coworkers was telling a friend about her recent haircut and she said, "Yeah, I really like that place. She did a great job. I had to trim the bangs a bit when I got home, but I really like the cut." Will she return to that beautician? Yes, she will, and she seems to be perfectly happy with less-than-excellent service. In answering customer satisfaction surveys, we tend to answer, "Satisfied" or "Extremely Satisfied" just to be nice, when we really wish the store had faster service and better lighting.

Don't be satisfied with "satisfied" customers. Us the *What If* worksheet to form customer-service policies that will thrill your customers. Dazzle them with your quality and service.

Worksheet: What If

What will you do when a client is angry or simply dissatisfied?
Remember, if they don't seem delighted, they might be unhappy but too
busy or polite to complain. If they are complaining, that's good. They are
providing information you *need*.

Consider what might happen to make a customer angry or simply
dissatisfied and come up with a solution that would make you happy if
you were the customer…even if the customer is *not* right. Your objective
is a happy customer!

Potential Problem	Amazingly wonderful solution *for your customer*

Adding New Products and Services

It is said that a business that is not growing is dying. Even if you decide to remain a very small part-time business, you should always be looking for new potential customers to replace the ones who will leave. But consider carefully before deciding to expand the products or services you offer. Too-quick growth has killed many businesses. You want to grow at a pace that is comfortable for you.

This might be a good time to use a brief questionnaire, or to add a question or two to your client-satisfaction questionnaire. If you are cleaning homes, leave a short questionnaire asking whether your client would use the following services if you decide to add them: Pick-up and delivery of dry cleaning or groceries; gift shopping and wrapping; car washing; yard work; general errands. Once you have some feedback, you can decide which services would be most in demand and most profitable.

You can also decide whether to provide such services yourself, or to contract them out. This might be a good time to expand your business, and start building a team of workers to provide services to your expanding customer base. (You will need to research the legal and tax requirements of employing others or using subcontractors.)

Use the following worksheet to list all possible add-on products and services. Then rule out the impractical ones, and survey your customers to discover the best way to grow.

Worksheet: Growing My Business

Use the mind-map method for this one. Write your business name or product/service in the center of the circle and then fill the other circles with whatever comes to mind.

Maybe *Daycare* will lead to brothers-and-sisters, potluck for families, and put-on-a-play.
Maybe *Business Writing* will lead to corporate authors, ghostwriting and anthologies. What if *Kitchen-tool Sales* leads to cooking classes and dinner-for-a-week chef services?

Let your mind wander as you jot down related ideas, and then reign it back in as you cross out impractical ideas, but watch out for that crazy idea that makes your heart skip a beat. It might be a goldmine.

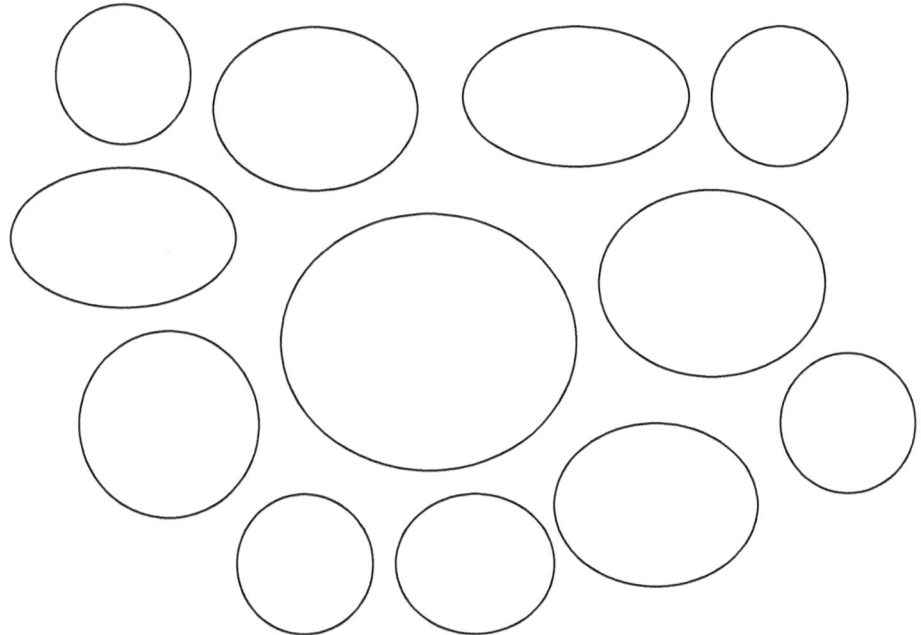

In-box

```
   From: Big Bad Boss
      To: You
Subject: Tuck these away

Wednesday would be a good mid-week point to
celebrate the progress you have made each
week.

Tuck these away somewhere for Wednesdays:

W  -  WONDER
E  -  ENDURANCE
D  -  DISCIPLINE
N  -  NAPS
E  -  ENDURANCE (get it?)
S  -  SATISFACTION, SUCCESS, SMILES
D  -  DISCIPLINE, DISCIPLINE, DISCIPLINE
A  -  ATTITUDE
Y  -  YOURS

Make today a great day!
```

There is more information in the appendices below. I wish you well, and I will assume the same good wishes from you. Let's stick with it, shall we? And encourage others along the way! God speed!

Appendix A: 65 Money-making Ideas

Creating an iPhone application is talked about like a new get-rich-quick scheme. Some people *have* made a lot of money, and others have built businesses around applications after they have proven successful. In at least one instance, new rules rendered the application almost worthless. If you are a developer, I do encourage you to be creative and come up with applications that fill needs or entertain, but before you run through all of your retirement income, you might need to provide a solid local service, too.

Use this list as a starting point to spark your own creative idea for part-time or potential full-time income. Keep in mind that tried-and-true ideas like home daycare and home or office cleaning are more likely to quickly generate income than some of the more creative ideas listed.

Add the following checklist items to your action plan before you get started making money, but please don't let these considerations stop you from accomplishing your goal. You can do all that is needed!

- What type of local business license or permit is needed?
- Is professional legal and/or financial advice needed to determine any insurance needs, liabilities, and so on?
- What additional skills or knowledge would you need?

This checklist does not suggest in any way that the business ideas here will be successful if tried. Too many factors are involved in running a profitable venture to predict the success of any idea. Once you have decided on a business venture, be sure to do the research necessary for your success.

If some of these ideas sound silly, a peanut-butter-and-jelly-sandwich restaurant sounds silly, but I read about one such successful venture. Success can't be guaranteed (so remember NOT to spend money you can't afford to lose), but it is a possibility if you use wisdom and give it all you've got. My best wishes for your success!

Craft and Art Ideas

Window Boxes - in a variety of colors to match your customer's home or apartment. The special touch -- you pre-plant them with a beautiful array of flowers.

Pillows - large and small, to fit any decorating need. Soft colors with lambs and bunnies could do very well as baby gifts.

Custom Accessories - a variety of coordinated scarves, belts, vests, socks and caps to turn one outfit into three or four. Conduct wardrobe-stretching workshops ("Look like a million bucks for just a few dollars") and sell them in sets.

Gift Baskets - filled with goodies. Specialize with a few themes or go all out for weddings, new babies, romantic evening, birthdays, Valentine's Day, and so on.

Signs & Banners - for businesses, parties, and parades.

Yard Sale Success - You place the ads, tack up the signs, set up the merchandise, and run the sale, possibly for a percentage of the profits. Specialize in neighborhood sales and fundraisers for organizations. For your do-it-yourself customers, sell a "Yard-Sale Success Kit" with signs and instructions.

Photography - Take informal shots of parties and graduations, etc. Let your customer choose the album cover, and arrange the photos attractively, with mementos, and leave room for customers to write their own captions under each photo. Offer digital photos for Web sites, too, if you have the equipment, or invest back into your business to purchase that equipment. (Make sure the camera you buy puts out the right quality for digital *and* print photos. Pictures may need to be a higher resolution, for instance, if they will be used in a local newspaper.)

Knitting, Sewing, Quilting - babies' and toddlers' smocks and simple jump suits, or designer fashions for all shapes and sizes ... or for hard-to-fit shapes and sizes.

Dollhouse Finishing - Offer your services to assemble the customer's dollhouse kit, and to decorate and furnish it. Buy and finish a few of your own to sell. Advertise your services in Nutshell News Magazine.

Calligraphy - Render your customers' favorite poems, or their wedding vows to be framed, and invitations, announcements, awards and certificates, in calligraphy. (Offer to illustrate them for an additional fee.)

Summer Kids' Craft Kits - for frantic Moms during hectic summer months. Box or bag simple crafts with instructions, or simply combine arts and crafts tools and supplies and let their imaginations fly. Or offer make-and-take craft workshops where you also offer your kits for sale. How about a Make-and-Take Crafty Birthday Party? You might be surprised at how much parents are willing to pay to make their little ones' birthdays unique and memorable.

Birdhouses - designed in colorful patterns, or make to attract specific types of birds. Put together a fun instructional sheet or booklet on how the whole family can enjoy feeding and spying on their feathered guests.

Flea Market / Craft Show Organizer - Rent half of a little-used parking lot (or ask the owners to let you use it in exchange for the increased traffic it will bring to their shops and restaurants). Charge participants a display-space fee. You will do the promotions to draw the crowd. Don't underestimate the cost and time involved in promotion, but don't get discouraged, either! Talk to organizers of similar events to learn what is needed. Your local newspaper advertising department can give you ideas, too. (Display advertising is usually completely separate from the classified advertising department, and employees in both departments might offer helpful advertising tips.)

Green-thumb Consultant - Many people who would enjoy gardening lack the time or the know-how to get started. Consult with your client about preferences and budget, and then plant the garden. Schedule follow-up visits until he or she can maintain it independently. Many folks who would never consider calling a landscaping firm might give a Green-thumb Consultant or a Backyard-Garden Planner a call.

Writing - There are many possibilities aside from traditional fiction and non-fiction publication in books and magazines. Investigate the possibility off writing and marketing your own newsletter, local cookbook or anthology. You are limited only by your talent and imagination, and by your marketing efforts and what the public will buy.

Flea Market Sales - Almost anything can be sold at flea markets, and you can even let your children take part. Whatever you decide to sell, reserve some space for your children to display their old toys or simple craft items or cookies they have made. Teach them the benefit of investing their allowance in a product to be sold at a profit, instead of simply spending it.

One couple I know shopped yard sales for great bargains, then rented a table at a flea market and sold the items at a good profit. Or, if you and a few friends each have your own talent, get together to split the cost of a table and display your items together. A crowded display table with a variety of products neatly arranged always seems to draw more of a crowd than a table displaying only pillows or hats, for instance.

Consign to Local Stores - Create whatever art or craft items you most enjoy. Market to local stores on consignment (they give you your share of profit from the pieces they sell, and they return the unsold items to you). Number and sign your creations to let your customers know they are limited editions or original creations.

Personal Service Ideas

Dinner Delivery - Establish accounts with two or three local restaurants, then advertise for customers to call you with their orders. You pick up the restaurant meal and deliver it to your customer. Your profit comes from a delivery fee paid by the customer, and/or from buying the meals at a discount that the restaurant is willing to give you in exchange for the added sales it will bring them.

Organizer - Reduce clutter! Specialize in closets, kitchens, offices, attics, or do it all.

Group-fun Tours - for singles or seniors, mother/daughter, father/son or mix and match. How about tours for housebound folks with a wheelchair-accessible vehicle? Require each person to come with an attendant if needed.

Chocolate Emergency Hotline - a sweet delivery service for those times when they just have to have something sweet right away. Specialize in unique varieties.

Box Lunches - Every weekday at lunchtime, an enterprising young woman visited one office where I worked with a teacart filled with wrapped sandwiches, fruit and cookies. And every day we lined up to pay her slightly high prices for the convenience of avoiding the fast food traffic jams outside.

Cleaning - Light cleaning, heavy cleaning, houses, apartments, offices, hourly, daily, weekly ... you decide. Be sure to charge enough to make the hard work worth your effort. Everyone I know who starts a business like this becomes busy fairly quickly and stays busy. The risk is that you get stuck doing this for life. Here's how it works: this pays fairly well, and of course you become dependent upon earning that weekly amount of money from cleaning x number of homes. Then, six years down the road when you become sick and tired of cleaning for a living, you decide to make a change, but the other jobs you are qualified for pay entry-level wages. If you are going to clean, be sure to make the time to train for another skill in your "spare" time, and plan to manage others, too. Learn the trade, get really good at it, and then employ others, keeping a portion of the fee charged but paying fair wages to the sub-contractors you work with, too.

Workspace Rental - Do you have an empty garage or spare room? Add a computer and printer or workbench and rent the space by the hour or by the day or week to local students, writers, artists, or other professionals.

Business Etiquette Training - Call it, "Getting Ahead in Corporate America; Doing it right" or something similarly upbeat. Teach high school and college students, as well as the already employed, how to survive and advance in today's business world. Personal grooming tips (if you want to move from secretary to manager, dress like a manager), as well as excellent written and verbal communication skills (such as listening skills) are essential, and too few people have mastered them. Make it fun!

Creative Dates - Come up with some unique afternoons and evenings out, or design local weekend get-aways for Moms and Dads, complete with planned activities for the kids who stay at home (the parents provide the babysitter, of course). Put together a few unique packages and have fun marketing your services. Examples might include hot-air ballooning; horseback riding; inner tubing; flight in an open-cockpit biplane; a limousine picnic; panning for gold; and restaurant hopping (appetizer in one restaurant, dinner in another and dessert at a third).

Childcare - Care for one to five children on a full-time basis, or simply organize a playgroup a few mornings or afternoons a week for "Mother's Morning Out." If space is a problem, offer to care for a working mother's child in her home, and provide that care for free in exchange for her allowing three or four additional children to be cared for in her home. You keep the profit, and she gets free day care ... everyone wins! Many local governments offer classes and guidelines on creating a contract for day-care clients to sign. You must decide whether parents pay even when their child is sick, and identify a back up for days when you are sick, if permitted by local regulations. You might want to specify that you get one paid week of vacation per year, too, since you will receive no benefits.

Tutoring - What is your specialty? Sports, dance, homework help, English or English-as-a-second-language, sewing, cooking ... you name it! If you love it, your students will be excited about it, too.

Computer Training - for adults and children, in very small groups or with individuals.

Birthday Party Entertainment - perform a clown act or puppet show at children's parties ... you can even use stuffed animals you already own as puppets. Just dress them up a bit. Do a lively reading of your favorite children's story, and give out small treats to top it off.

Business Service Ideas

Plant Service - You provide and care for the plants in your clients' offices. You would provide vibrant, healthy plants and care for them weekly for a flat monthly rate. If they wither, you replace them. Provide a few facts on how plants in the workplace help to reduce stress and increase cooperation.

Equipment Rental - tools, computers...whatever you have, rent it out and put part of the profits into more inventory to help your business grow. Give each customer a questionnaire to help you identify other items to offer for rent.

Answering Service - Get a business phone line and have your clients put their phones on "call forwarding" to your number when they are out. (Call forwarding is offered by most phone companies.)

Office Workouts - an invigorating exercise class...at the office. Make it fun. Offer to charge the business owner, who can then offer the classes as an employee benefit, or charge the individual attendees. Free custom tee shirts are a great promotional item, or sell them. A variation of this idea is to offer the services of a Personal Trainer, meeting with one client at a time, several times a week, in their offices or homes. Of course, as with many of these ideas, licenses and certificates must probably be obtained, as well as liability insurance.

Real Estate Service - Real Estate agents have many small jobs to do for each home they sell. Offer your services to put in and remove sighs, clean empty houses, mow lawns of vacant homes, and rent out light furnishings to help empty houses sell more quickly.

Business Writer - You can market your writing skills to local businesses and organizations to produce routine business letters, sales letters, company newsletters, instruction manuals, brochures and advertising. (If you enjoy writing ad copy, log onto thewellfedwriter.com or read the book by the same name.

Miscellaneous Ideas

Here, my list of moneymaking ideas continues. I am sure you can add to this list with a little research and imagination. After all, perhaps you are alive to contribute something *only you* can contribute. Customize these ideas with a touch of *you*.

Typing/word processing	Executive errand service
Research service	House or pet sitting
Carpet/furniture cleaning	Window washing
Small appliance repair	Paper hanging
Aerobics instructor	Elder care
Seamstress/alterations	Videotape events
Career-change consultant	Bookkeeper
Fashion consultant	Bed & breakfast
Shopping service	Graphic artist
Home-office Set-up	Wedding planner
Job search assistance/resume	Meeting/event planner
Music lessons	Catering
Yard services	Apartment finder

Multi-level or Direct Sales Companies

There are some who say that the only people who make money in direct sales companies are those at the top, but I know men, women and families who earn extra cash or a solid income with various companies. I know more people who make a little money and quit, after investing hours and hours in the business. I have never met anyone who said they wish they never got involved. The sales training and encouragement you receive are typically great benefits of working with these companies, and you get to meet some really great people.

So use wisdom, don't spend money you can't afford to lose, follow your gut, have fun and work hard!

I sold Avon products between jobs, and I still use and recommend their products. Typically, the investment required to get started is $15 for a starter kit that provides you with brochures and sample products. See Avon.com or contact Maria in New York at mariaavon@aol.com.

Tupperware and Pampered Chef are two more very reputable companies to consider if you are thinking about this method of business.

Multi-level or network marketing companies sell everything from cosmetics and image consulting to vitamins, clothing, toys, educational products, and chocolate, as well as big-ticket items like water purification systems, home security systems, and even executive training seminars.

Each company has its own rules, policies and procedures. You are usually paid a commission on what you sell, as well as a bonus or commission for what is sold by anyone who agrees to work with you in the organization, in exchange for helping to train and motivate those people.

Some of these companies require you to purchase your initial stock of merchandise and some do not. Some companies require you to deliver the merchandise to your customers, and some ship directly to the customer. Some companies provide initial training, and some do not, but almost all of these companies conduct regular meetings to train and motivate their sales force. Most sell their products at home parties and some also are sold by catalog and online, but you are still your own boss. You set your own hours and establish your own income goals.

There are many exciting opportunities out there, but you will want to be sure that any company you are considering working with is legitimate and that you feel comfortable with its sales philosophy. Be sure to carefully consider the time commitment if you have to deliver products yourself. If you are going to shoot for a specific target income, have someone already in the organization help you estimate how many sales you will need per week or per month to reach your goal.

The motivation and encouragement these companies offer is an essential ingredient in any business effort, but try not to be overly optimistic. Too-high expectations for success can lead to disappointment when you have been working for two long years and are still making the equivalent of less-than-minimum wage. On the other hand, if you put in the hours and do the work (following *their* plan), you can make an excellent income while offering that same work-for-yourself opportunity to others.

Appendix B: Resources for Your Business

Take advantage of these resources, but don't get lost among them. There are so many resources online – you probably already know how easy it is to be distracted from your objective by clicking on one interesting resource or news item after another.

If you are new to the online world, establish this habit early on: accomplish what you plan to get done and then close the browser and get back to work!

Microsoft's Template Gallery Microsoft offers templates you can personalize for everything from cover letters to resumes (for that ongoing job hunt), cookbooks to business surveys, project management templates to party invitations, and spreadsheets to presentations. http://office.microsoft.com/en-us/templates/default.aspx
Press-Release-Writing.com This is an excellent source with a free press-release template and how-to information on writing and distributing press releases to publicize your business effort. Sign up for their free newsletter but *first*, **re-read the chapter in this book titled, "Special Section: Publicity!"** http://www.Press-Release-Writing.com
Jim Blasingame: Small Business Advocate Take advantage of resources at his Web site and sign up for his free e-mail newsletter. http://www.smallbusinessadvocate.com

US Chamber of Commerce
See their "Small Business How-to" section and sign up for their free e-mail newsletter.

http://www.uschamber.com

1099: The Magazine for Independent Professionals (archives only)
This site mentions that they are no longer updating the Web site, but archives are available and are very much worth reading.

http://www.1099.com

Your printing needs
VistaPrint offers full-color business cards free (certain designs). Just pay the low shipping cost.

http://www.VistaPrint.com

My local printer, Zebra Print Solutions, provides excellent service very affordably and can work with you no matter where you live.

http://www.zebraprintsolutions.com

SCORE
The Senior Corps of Retired Executives (SCORE) provides short counseling sessions, free and anonymous, to help people understand aspects of starting a new business. In many areas you will be able to find a local office, or you can contact them online.

http://www.SCORE.org

Small Business Development Center This arm of the government's Small Business Administration (SBA) is devoted to start-up companies. http://www.sba.gov/sbdc
Local Business Incubation Centers and Business Development Centers Many community colleges and chambers of commerce offer classes (often free of charge) to local residents who need information on starting a very small business. A few phone calls should tell you whether there is such a service in your area.
Ten Golden Rules Jay Berkowitz, founder and CEO of Ten Golden Rules, was one instructor in an online marketing course I took recently. His company provides Internet marketing consultation and offers a free newsletter, exclusive interviews via podcast, solid encouragement plus much, much more. http://tengoldenrules.com

As you locate resources online, if you can't resist clicking from site to site to site, set a timer and stop when it rings, or limit yourself to accomplish one or two tasks, then look at one or two sites for fun and then GET BACK TO WORK.

In-box

From: Big Bad Boss
  To: You
Subject: Three Quick Things

As you work on your project or look for a job and/or start your small business, what three quick things can you do to encourage yourself today?

1. Write down *two* things you've already done and one new thing and then start checking them off.

2. Redecorate (if you are a man, make that "clean") one corner of your living/working area to give your eyes a beautiful place to rest.

3. Instead of big things first, try the small-things-first method I read about. Take care of a few little tasks so they won't bother you daily and distract you from the big ones.

Do the above *or* make up your own three fast things to do and GET TO WORK.

Appendix C: Kick in the Pants

We could all use some tough love from time to time, especially when it comes to self-discipline. So read one entry below, and then PUT DOWN THIS BOOK AND GET OVER TO THAT DESK. Start working to be your own boss TODAY. Go to my Yahoo KickInThePants group for more messages. Here are a few I selected for you. (http://Groups.Yahoo.com/Group/KickinThePants)

Good Morning!

I'm so glad you are honorable and reliable -- WHEN IT COMES TO OTHER PEOPLE. What about YOU?

Why do *you* come last? I'm not talking about rewards and little kindnesses. I hope you treat yourself well. I'm talking about WORK.

You work for others. You show up and you get it done. WHY, when it comes to working for yourself, DO YOU BECOME A SLACKER?

If you arrived to do a job for someone else, and you sat down in front of the nearest television and watched three shows, how would that look?

You wouldn't do it to them. DON'T DO IT TO YOURSELF.

We need downtime, but we must put our work-for-ourselves time FIRST. Work a little, play a little.

Quit setting unrealistic goals. Make them do-able, AND THEN DO THEM. Give yourself the same honorable treatment that you give others. WHEN YOU SHOW UP FOR WORK (on your project), WORK, BABY.

Then give yourself a tiny reward and a big grin and do it again tomorrow.

Signing Off,
Big Bad Boss

Good Morning!

Admit it. If the TV weren't in the room, you wouldn't watch it. If my current project was easier to get to than my computer, I would SIT DOWN AND GET SOME WORK DONE instead of reading online news headlines and watching video after video.

In my house, we've taken care of the TV thing -- no televisions in the house for the past few years – but the computer has taken the television's place. The kids even discovered Sponge Bob episodes on there ... need I say more?

So I'm going to move this computer and replace it with my project. You do the same, OK?

Find the culprit. What is keeping you from getting important work done?

DEAL WITH IT.

Signing Off,
Big Bad Boss

Good Morning,

When you are changing direction, make sure it's a change and not a cop out. If you are abandoning a project, ask yourself why.

1. If fear is your inspiration, STOMP ON IT AND GET BACK TO WORK.
2. If procrastination is the cause, KILL IT AND MOVE FORWARD.
3. If a change in goals and/or priorities is the cause, pat yourself on the back and set goals that reflect your new direction.

If you chose #1 or #2 above, do some reading on the fear of failure, fear of success, procrastination and its causes, and how to overcome it.

If you chose #3, BON VOYAGE! Don't look back.

Signing Off,
Big Bad Boss

Hey!

It's two in the morning. *What are you doing up?*

When you are up in the middle of the night, GET SOME WORK DONE ON YOUR PROJECT OR GO TO SLEEP.

Don't read and write e-mails. AND DON'T GO WATCH TV, EITHER. Get at least a little bit done on your project.

Hey – *quit reading that novel*! I see you! Quit consuming others' work and CREATE SOMETHING OF YOUR OWN.

Take advantage of "found" time. It adds up.

Signing Off,
Big Bad Boss

Appendix D: God and You

I don't have the answers. And if I say that God has the answers, that might not help you much if you've been asking and asking God for help, and nothing has changed.

The wisdom of the Bible, which world leaders and moms and dads and grandparents and young people around the world have relied on for over a thousand years, can breathe life into your breathless spirit as you wait on God for answers that only He can see.

I believe God gives us our talents and abilities. Whether you think they come from God or nature, it is clear that we each have strengths in certain areas. I have always been able to write clearly, but you would be very sorry if you had to listen to me sing. My sister and my daughter can sketch and draw, but you might not really enjoy a meal they would prepare (don't tell them I wrote that, OK?).

Go Ahead and Ask

Pray and ask God which service you should provide. Just bow your head and lay down your pride to say, "Lord, I will clean toilets or become a famous artist. Whatever You want, I am willing to do. You can see my heart…please help me feel as I should. Help me deal with any self-pity, anger, pride or greed that gets in my way. Amen!"

Cry out to God for the things you don't have. If there isn't enough food or rent/mortgage money, love or joy or peace, then get alone with God and *cry out*. If you are in America with me, you might have to learn that it is OK to truly cry out – I mean holler and wail – and let God know you hurt. Allow yourself to know you hurt and then trust God to heal you. (Read a few psalms and listen to King David as he cried out to God during times when he was being persecuted unjustly *and* after times of his own betraying and murderous acts.)

Practice thankfulness for the things you *do* have. If you have family or friends, hot and cold running water, good health, if you live in a free country, have a car that works, or a couch to sit on – whatever you *do* have, thank God for those things. Take a deep breath and rest in God's care while you are doing the dishes or mowing the lawn. Watch your life take on a whole new aspect as you relax a bit and rely on God's care.

Allow me to show you, with all due respect to other belief systems, the mental picture I get when I talk with folks who say we should "trust the universe" to meet our needs: You walk up to the stove and tell it, "I'd like chicken and dumplings for dinner tonight," while the chef stands by, unseen and unasked, thinking, "Is she talking to the *stove*?" And our Father God the Creator, unseen and unasked, thinks, "Is she talking to *nature*?"

I spent over half my life thinking God wasn't real, so I know very well what that feels like. If you have had a less-than-good experience with the Christian church in America or elsewhere, please don't hold that against God. He is perfect; we are *not*. Religion can be defined as people following rules. Faith is a *relationship*, and a personal intimate relationship with God is possible through prayer and reading His word.

"'I know the plans I have for you,' declares the LORD, 'plans to prosper you and not to harm you, plans to give you hope and a future.'" [1] If you need His help right now, please simply stop and pray. Ask Him to be in charge of your life and thank Him for sending His son to die for your sins. You may or may not feel different, but if you pray that sincerely, your spirit will be new and you will have the Comforter, the Holy Spirit of God, the same power by which Jesus rose again, living within you. Find a Bible-believing, Bible-teaching church and other Christians who will help you walk the walk and watch your life and your *self* change! It is *amazing*.

---

[1] **Jeremiah 29: 11 – 12** "For I know the plans I have for you," declares the LORD, "plans to prosper you and not to harm you, plans to give you hope and a future. Then you will call upon me and come and pray to me, and I will listen to you."

And, if you already believe in God but you haven't noticed His help, pray and ask Him to help you truly know and love Him more. Read an easier-to-understand version of the Bible a bit every day, praying for understanding. I promise this formula can radically change your life. God will radically change you from the inside out, and He will become more real to you than a close friend here on earth.

You are God's kid. Pray away!

May God speed you on your way toward earning the money you need, and enough to share!

www.ingramcontent.com/pod-product-compliance
Lightning Source LLC
Chambersburg PA
CBHW051541170526
45165CB00002B/835